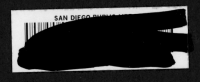

D0852357

SHERMAN'S MARCH
Atlanta to the Sea

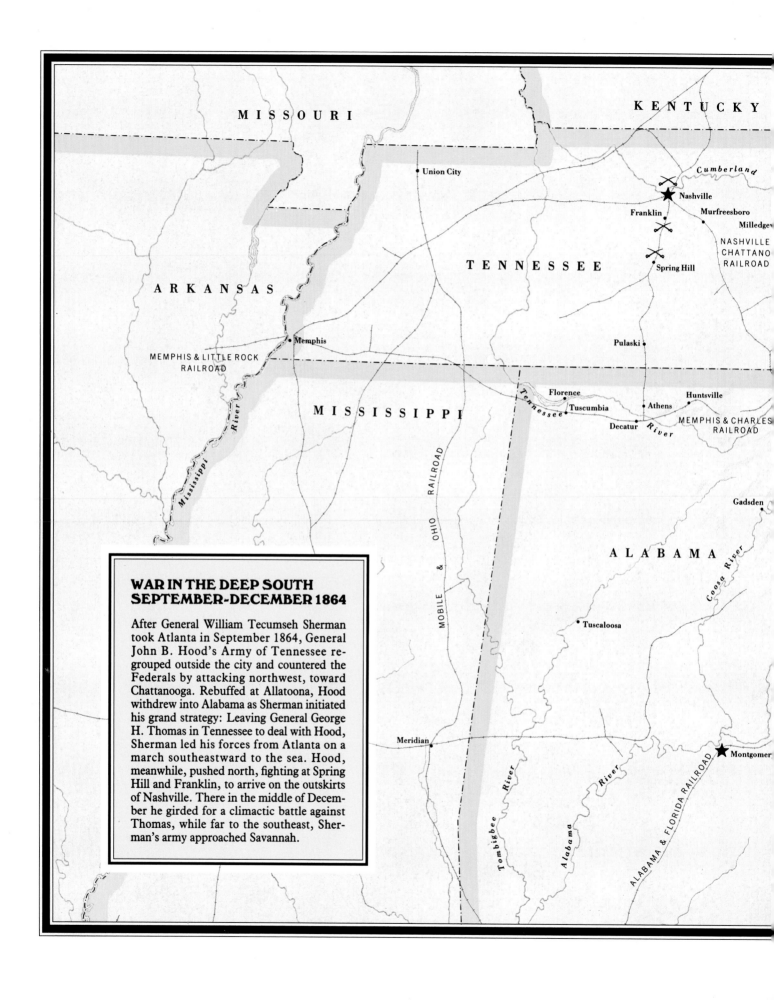

MISSOURI

KENTUCKY

• Union City

Cumberland

ARKANSAS

⚔ ★ Nashville

Franklin ⚔
Murfreesboro

Milledge•

TENNESSEE

⚔

NASHVILLE
CHATTANO
RAILROAD

• Spring Hill

Pulaski •

• Memphis

MEMPHIS & LITTLE ROCK
RAILROAD

MISSISSIPPI

Florence •
Tuscumbia •

Huntsville •

• Athens

Decatur •

Tennessee

River

MEMPHIS & CHARLES
RAILROAD

Mississippi River

Gadsden •

Coosa River

ALABAMA

RAILROAD

• Tuscaloosa

OHIO

&

MOBILE

WAR IN THE DEEP SOUTH
SEPTEMBER-DECEMBER 1864

After General William Tecumseh Sherman
took Atlanta in September 1864, General
John B. Hood's Army of Tennessee re-
grouped outside the city and countered the
Federals by attacking northwest, toward
Chattanooga. Rebuffed at Allatoona, Hood
withdrew into Alabama as Sherman initiated
his grand strategy: Leaving General George
H. Thomas in Tennessee to deal with Hood,
Sherman led his forces from Atlanta on a
march southeastward to the sea. Hood,
meanwhile, pushed north, fighting at Spring
Hill and Franklin, to arrive on the outskirts
of Nashville. There in the middle of December he girded for a climactic battle against
Thomas, while far to the southeast, Sherman's army approached Savannah.

Meridian •

★ Montgomer•

Tombigbee River

Alabama River

ALABAMA & FLORIDA RAILROAD

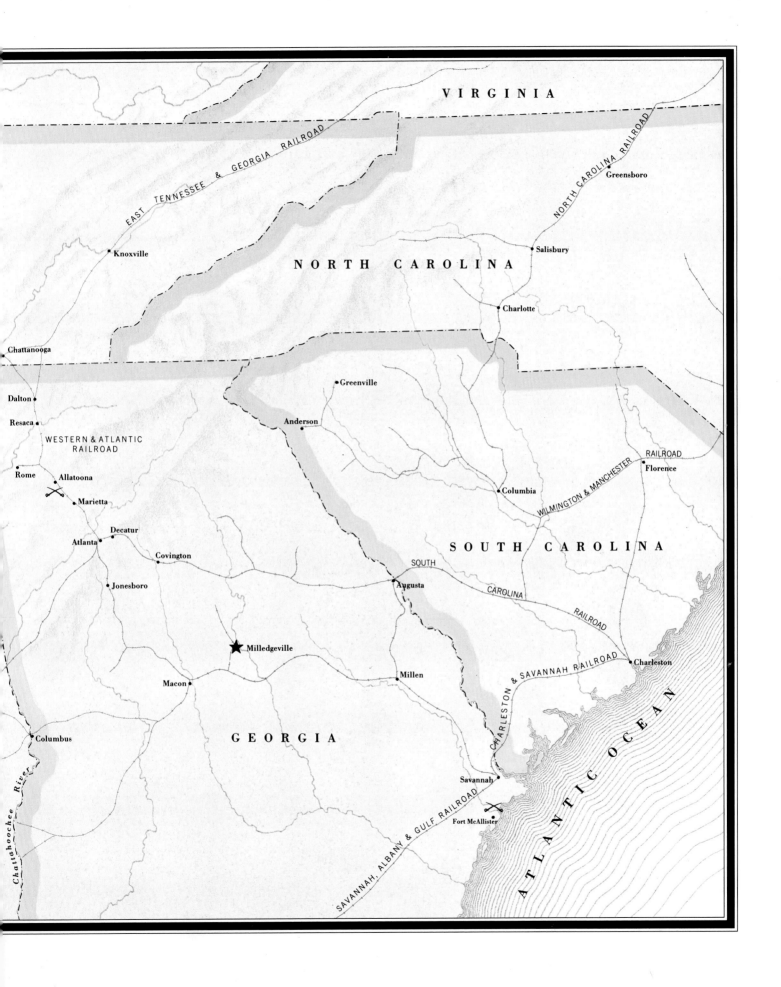

This volume is one of a series that chronicles in full the
events of the American Civil War, 1861-1865.
Other books in the series include:

The Cover: Major General William Tecumseh
Sherman, on a black horse, rides with his staff past a
group of freed slaves in this painting of Sherman's
march to the sea by artist A. J. Carlin. The wholesale
destruction of the land's resources by Sherman's
troops spread a sense of helplessness through the
Confederacy, portending the end of the War.

THE
CIVIL
WAR

SHERMAN'S MARCH

BY

DAVID NEVIN

AND THE

EDITORS OF TIME-LIFE BOOKS

Atlanta to the Sea

TIME-LIFE BOOKS, ALEXANDRIA, VIRGINIA

Time-Life Books Inc.
is a wholly owned subsidiary of

TIME INCORPORATED

FOUNDER: Henry R. Luce 1898-1967

Editor-in-Chief: Henry Anatole Grunwald
Chairman and Chief Executive Officer: J. Richard Munro
President and Chief Operating Officer: N. J. Nicholas Jr.
Chairman of the Executive Committee: Ralph P. Davidson
Corporate Editor: Ray Cave
Executive Vice President, Books: Kelso F. Sutton
Vice President, Books: George Artandi

TIME-LIFE BOOKS INC.

EDITOR: George Constable
Executive Editor: Ellen Phillips
Director of Design: Louis Klein
Director of Editorial Resources: Phyllis K. Wise
Editorial Board: Russell B. Adams Jr., Dale M. Brown,
Roberta Conlan, Thomas H. Flaherty, Lee Hassig,
Donia Ann Steele, Rosalind Stubenberg,
Kit van Tulleken, Henry Woodhead
Director of Photography and Research:
John Conrad Weiser

PRESIDENT: Christopher T. Linen
Chief Operating Officer: John M. Fahey Jr.
Senior Vice Presidents: James L. Mercer,
Leopoldo Toralballa
Vice Presidents: Stephen L. Bair, Ralph J. Cuomo, Neal
Goff, Stephen L. Goldstein, Juanita T. James, Hallett
Johnson III, Carol Kaplan, Susan J. Maruyama, Robert
H. Smith, Paul R. Stewart, Joseph J. Ward
Director of Production Services: Robert J. Passantino

The Civil War

Series Director: Henry Woodhead
Designers: Susan K. White, Edward Frank
Series Administrator: Philip Brandt George

Editorial Staff for *Sherman's March*
Associate Editors: David S. Thomson (text);
Marion F. Briggs (pictures)
Staff Writers: Stephen G. Hyslop, John Newton,
Daniel Stashower
Researchers: Susan V. Kelly, Stephanie Lewis
(principals); Harris J. Andrews, Patti H. Cass,
Mark Moss, Brian C. Pohanka
Copy Coordinator: Jayne E. Rohrich
Picture Coordinator: Betty H. Weatherley
Editorial Assistant: Donna Fountain
Special Contributors: Elissa E. Baldwin, Mimi Harrison,
Brian McGinn

Editorial Operations
Copy Chief: Diane Ullius
Editorial Operations Manager: Caroline A. Boubin
Production: Celia Beattie
Quality Control: James J. Cox (director)
Library: Louise D. Forstall

Correspondents: Elisabeth Kraemer-Singh (Bonn);
Maria Vincenza Aloisi (Paris); Ann Natanson (Rome).
Valuable assistance was also provided by Carolyn Chubet
(New York).

Library of Congress Cataloguing in Publication Data
Nevin, David, 1927-
    Sherman's march.
    (The Civil War)
    Bibliography: p.
    Includes index.
    1. Sherman's March to the Sea.   I. Time-Life Books.
II. Title.   III. Series.
E476.69.N48 1986   973.7'378   86-5764
ISBN 0-8094-4812-2
ISBN 0-8094-4813-0 (lib. bdg.)

The Author:
David Nevin, a writer for *Life* for 10 years, is a veteran
Time-Life Books author. He wrote two volumes in The
Epic of Flight library, four in The Old West series, among
them *The Soldiers* and *The Mexican War*, as well as *The
Road to Shiloh* in The Civil War series. He is also the
author of *Dream West*, a historical novel based on the career of John Charles Frémont, the noted Western explorer
and Civil War general.

The Consultants:
Colonel John R. Elting, USA (Ret.), a former Associate
Professor at West Point, is the author of *Battles for Scandi-
navia* in the Time-Life Books World War II series and of
*The Battle of Bunker's Hill, The Battles of Saratoga, Mili-
tary History and Atlas of the Napoleonic Wars, American
Army Life* and *The Superstrategists.* Co-author of *A Dictionary of Soldier Talk*, he is also editor of the three volumes of *Military Uniforms in America, 1755-1867*, and associate editor of *The West Point Atlas of American Wars.*

William A. Frassanito, a Civil War historian and lecturer
specializing in photograph analysis, is the author of two
award-winning studies, *Gettysburg: A Journey in Time* and
*Antietam: The Photographic Legacy of America's Bloodiest
Day*, and a companion volume, *Grant and Lee, The Virginia Campaigns.* He has also served as chief consultant to the
photographic history series *The Image of War.*

Les Jensen, Director of the Second Armored Division
Museum, Fort Hood, Texas, specializes in Civil War arti-
facts and is a conservator of historic flags. He is a contribu-
tor to *The Image of War* series, consultant for numerous
Civil War publications and museums, and a member of
the Company of Military Historians. He was formerly Curator of the U.S. Army Transportation Museum at Fort
Eustis, Virginia, and before that Curator of the Museum
of the Confederacy in Richmond, Virginia.

Michael McAfee specializes in military uniforms and has
been Curator of Uniforms and History at the West Point
Museum since 1970. A fellow of the Company of Military
Historians, he coedited with Colonel Elting *Long Endure:
The Civil War Years*, and he collaborated with Frederick
Todd on *American Military Equipage.* He is the author of
Artillery of the American Revolution, 1775-1783, and has
written numerous articles for *Military Images Magazine.*

James P. Shenton, Professor of History at Columbia University, is a specialist in 19th-century American political
and social history, with particular emphasis on the Civil
War period. He is the author of *Robert John Walker* and
Reconstruction South.

CONTENTS

The Union's Avenging Angel

In November 1864, when Major General William Tecumseh Sherman burned Atlanta and began his march to the sea, his name became synonymous with ruthless warfare. Northerners saw him as an avenging angel; to Southerners, he seemed nothing less than the devil himself.

In appearance, Sherman was as rough as his reputation. He was tall and sinewy, with a seamed, weather-beaten face, unkempt hair and scraggly red beard. He wore a threadbare uniform that was stained with nicotine. "He talked incessantly, giving orders, dictating telegrams, bright and chipper," a fellow officer observed.

Sherman's disdain for spit and polish sat well with his troops, who affectionately called him "Uncle Billy." He thought nothing of swimming naked in rivers and warming by his campfire at night, dressed in red flannel drawers and a worn dressing gown.

But as much as Sherman's taste and manners were democratic, his outlook was aristocratic. Sherman equated democracy with mob rule. He blamed the politicians for starting the War, even though his foster father, Thomas Ewing *(below, right)* and brother, John, were both U.S. Senators.

Sherman's allegiance was to law and order and to the Union. Having lived six years in the South before the War, he accepted slavery, however morally repugnant, as a legally established institution. To him, secession was the South's great sin and Southerners who supported the Confederacy deserved to be treated like criminals. "To those who submit to rightful authority, all gentleness and forbearance," he proclaimed. "But to petulant and persistent secessionists, why death is mercy and the quicker he or she is disposed of the better."

This coat of arms with the Latin motto Nothing without God was painted for Sherman's grandfather, Taylor Sherman, a distinguished jurist of Norwalk, Connecticut.

CHARLES ROBERT SHERMAN

THOMAS EWING

When Sherman's father *(far left)*, an Ohio Supreme Court judge, died in 1829, the nine-year-old boy was adopted by family friend Thomas Ewing *(near left)*, an up-and-coming lawyer in Lancaster, Ohio. When Ewing became a U.S. Senator, he appointed young Sherman to West Point.

From a low hill, Sherman watches his troops tramp along a winding Georgia road. He believed that maneuverability won battles and sought to mold his army "into a mobile machine."

En route by ship to California from New York in 1847, Sherman made this sketch of the harbor at Rio de Janeiro, one of the ports of call on the 198-day voyage. He toured the city with another young lieutenant, his friend and future commanding officer, Henry W. Halleck.

In 1855 Sherman sketched his home in San Francisco on the back of a check issued by the bank he headed. When the bank failed, the house and lot became, he said, "dead losses."

An Unsettled Life

Sherman's prewar career took so many turns that he once claimed to be "cursed to live a vagabond life." After graduating sixth in the West Point class of 1840, he served at army posts mainly in the South and in California. Unhappy with the low pay, he resigned his commission in 1853 to run a bank in San Francisco. When the bank failed in the financial panic of 1857, he found work in a bank in New York. It too failed. Sherman then moved to Leavenworth, Kansas, and became a lawyer. In January 1860, he took the post of superintendent of a new military school in Alexandria, Louisiana. One year later, Louisiana withdrew from the Union. In a letter of resignation, Sherman regretfully declared: "The consequence is inevitable — War and ugly war. The storm is upon us, and we must each to our own ship."

Sherman's eye for topography is evident in this map he drew of Monterey, California, his post during the Mexican War. He resented being assigned to a backwater while his peers fought in Mexico. In a letter home, he wrote: "Whilst I have been here where all is peace, others are gaining their experience that will make them our future generals."

This painting shows Sherman as superintendent of the Louisiana Seminary of Learning *(upper right)* in 1860. He was recommended for the position by his friends — and future foes — Braxton Bragg, Richard Taylor and P.G.T. Beauregard.

ELLEN EWING SHERMAN

WILLIAM TECUMSEH SHERMAN

MARIA BOYLE EWING SHERMAN
(MINNIE)

MARY ELIZABETH SHERMAN
(LIZZIE)

WILLIAM TECUMSEH SHERMAN JR.
(WILLY)

RACHEL EWING AND
ELEANOR MARY SHERMAN

A Devoted Father

In May of 1850, Sherman married Ellen Ewing, daughter of his foster father, Senator Thomas Ewing. The marriage was strained from the start. Ellen wanted her husband to embrace her Roman Catholic faith and to live quietly, close by her parents, in their hometown of Lancaster, Ohio. But Sherman spurned Catholicism and declined to settle down.

Only their mutual love for their children held the marriage together. Ellen bore him eight in all (six of whom are pictured here). The children brought out Sherman's gentler side. His favorite was his oldest son and namesake, William Tecumseh Jr.

In 1863, tragedy struck the family. Elated by the capture of Vicksburg in July, Sherman urged Ellen to visit him at his camp there with the four oldest children. During the happy reunion, Willy, aged nine, caught typhoid fever and died. The death devastated Sherman. Although his subsequent campaigns in Tennessee and Georgia made him famous, he cared little for the recognition. He confessed to Ellen: "With Willy dies in me all real ambition."

In Atlanta, on the evening before he began his march to the sea, he wrote his second son, Tommy *(below, right):* "People write to me that I am a great general, and if I were to come home they would gather round me and play music. That is what people call fame and glory, but I tell you that I would rather come down quietly and have you and Willy meet me at the car than to have the shouts of the people."

Sherman frequently wrote letters to his children, often enclosing souvenirs and sketches of places he and his troops had been. Above left is his drawing of the officers' mess tent on the Big Black River, near Vicksburg, Mississippi; at right, a scene of Federal guns at Vicksburg.

Seated in front of a map of the South, Sherman clasps his son Thomas Ewing Sherman, known as Tommy. Sherman did not want his boys to become soldiers; he thought a military career was "too full of blind chances."

13

The Enemies in Georgia

"We are all in the bright glow of victory, happy as lovers in their honeymoon, and ready to follow Sherman and Thomas to the ends of the Confederacy."

MAJOR JAMES CONNOLLY, FEDERAL XIV CORPS, IN ATLANTA

1

The Federal army that began marching into Atlanta on September 2, 1864, was galvanized by victory. One of the first major units to pass through the abandoned Confederate earthworks — the 1st Brigade of the 1st Division of the veteran XX Corps — swung down a city thoroughfare lustily singing a favorite ditty: "We will hang Jeff Davis on a sour apple tree." Bands played as more divisions came into the city over the next several days, and kept playing, by order of the commanding general, William Tecumseh Sherman. "Their music," Sherman recalled with delight, "was to us all a source of infinite pleasure during our sojourn." Reviews were held almost every day, the various units marching proudly in front of the redheaded commander whom the veterans had nicknamed Uncle Billy.

The troops had good reason to celebrate. They had survived a long, difficult campaign — four months of maneuvering and fighting across 130 miles of northwestern Georgia's rugged hills — and they had succeeded in flushing the enemy from the Confederacy's most important city after Richmond. The campaign had cost the Federal army far fewer casualties than might have been expected, thanks to Sherman's repeated flanking movements that had levered the Confederate defenders from one strong point after another and had finally forced them to abandon Atlanta itself. The Federal troops anticipated further triumphs under Uncle Billy, but for the moment they were looking forward to a period of rest and full rations. "We felt perfectly at home" in Atlanta, Sherman later wrote. "We had uninterrupted communications with the rear. The trains arrived with regularity and dispatch, and brought us ample supplies."

The capture of Atlanta did far more, of course, than give the army a chance to enjoy what Sherman quaintly termed "a period of repose." It put out of business one of the Confederacy's most important supply centers and it severed vital Southern rail links. Moreover, Sherman's successful campaign electrified the North, giving its war-weary people renewed faith that the conflict could be won. This scuttled the Democratic Party, whose peace platform in effect offered the Confederacy its independence, and made President Lincoln's reelection in November a near certainty. The War would continue.

Sherman was proud of his accomplishment, but he was also aware that it had placed him and his army in a precarious position. He was deep in enemy territory with more than 80,000 men to feed and supply, his life line a single railroad track running more than 300 miles back through Chattanooga to Nashville, Tennessee. That life line was all too vulnerable to slashing attacks carried out by Confederate cavalry raiders led by Generals Joseph Wheeler and Nathan Bedford Forrest. "I've got my wedge in pretty deep," Sherman told a friend, "and must look out that I don't get my fingers pinched."

This leather-covered brass telescope belonged to Lieutenant James H. Connelly of the 37th Indiana, who, on October 5, 1864, used it to read a signal flag message from a besieged garrison at Allatoona, Georgia, pleading for help. In reply, Connelly sent the message from General William T. Sherman that came to be immortalized as "Hold the fort, I am coming."

To help make Atlanta a more efficient and more easily defended military base, Sherman decided that it was necessary to evacuate all civilians. During the first week of September he informed those residents who had not already fled the city that they had to pack what they could and leave.

The order struck the Atlantans like a thunderbolt. Mayor James M. Calhoun and his fellow councilmen protested, saying that the results of an evacuation would be "appalling and heartrending." General John Bell Hood, whose Confederate army had withdrawn 30 miles south of Atlanta to Lovejoy's Station, was also appalled by Sherman's edict. When Sherman requested that Hood do his part to help pass Atlanta's refugees through the Confederate lines, the commander responded angrily with bitter accusations. Sherman's ploy, Hood wrote, was uncivilized — it constituted "studied and ingenious cruelty."

The protests elicited from Sherman a series of eloquent replies. He wrote to Hood that he had sound military reasons for his action. Leaving a large number of civilians in a captured city meant that he would be obliged to maintain a large garrison to control and protect them; this would have the effect of weakening the victorious army. Furthermore, Sherman noted, allowing civilians to remain where they might again be placed in the line of fire was hardly a humane proceeding.

But more important to Sherman was a broader issue. The Confederacy had begun the conflict, he said, and was responsible for all subsequent bloodshed. "You cannot qualify war in harsher terms than I will," he passionately told the mayor and his council. "War is cruelty and you cannot refine it; and those who brought war into our country deserve all the curses and maledictions a people can pour out." One might as well "appeal against the thunder-storm as against these terrible hardships of war," Sherman continued. "They are inevitable, and the only way the people of Atlanta can hope once more to live in peace and quiet at home, is to stop the war." For now the civilians had to leave, "until the mad passions of men cool down." In the end, 446 families were evacuated in an orderly fashion.

Having secured Atlanta to his satisfaction, Sherman still had to confront the most dangerous threat to his position — the Confederate army at Lovejoy's Station. That army of almost 40,000 troops, commanded by the exceedingly aggressive Hood, had slipped through Sherman's grasp during the last fighting around the city. At the moment, Hood seemed to be resting and reorganizing his force, but Sherman knew the fiery Kentuckian too well to entertain any illusions that he would remain inactive for long. Hood was sure to move in some direction, probably sooner rather than later, and the result was certain to cause trouble.

As Sherman contemplated his predicament, his fertile mind came up with the most unconventional and daring of all possible solutions. He could not afford to stay on the defensive, he told his most trusted subordinate, Major General George Thomas, "simply holding Atlanta and fighting for the safety of its railroad." Far better to confound the enemy by resuming the offensive. He would march his army across Georgia, in the direction of Savannah on the Atlantic Coast. If Hood followed, so much the better. The Federals had already beaten him three times around Atlanta and they could do it again.

Sherman planned to move too fast to maintain communication with his bases of supply. His troops would have to live off the land as they marched. "Where a million of people find subsistence, my army won't starve," Sherman wrote his commander, Ulysses S. Grant, in a dispatch explaining his scheme. Sherman told Grant that the army would be strong enough to outfight any force the Confederates could throw in its path. And nothing would more demoralize the Confederacy than to find an entire Federal army cutting a swath across the Southern heartland. His plan was certain to succeed, Sherman assured Grant, ending on a jocular personal note: "If you can whip Lee and I can march to the Atlantic, I think Uncle Abe will give us twenty days' leave of absence to see the young folks. Yours as ever."

Thus was hatched one of the most famous and dramatic marches in history. Eighteen years earlier, during the Mexican War, Winfield Scott had successfully undertaken a similar feat when he abandoned his base at Vera Cruz and advanced inland to Mexico City. European military men had watched that epic march with fascinated disbelief. Now another American general was preparing to set out on an equally unorthodox and risky journey.

Before Sherman could put his grand design into operation, he received word that

Residents of Atlanta load their belongings onto wagons provided by the Union army as they prepare to leave the city. Sherman's order gave the Atlantans 10 days to evacuate their homes, "to return," wrote one saddened resident, "perhaps never."

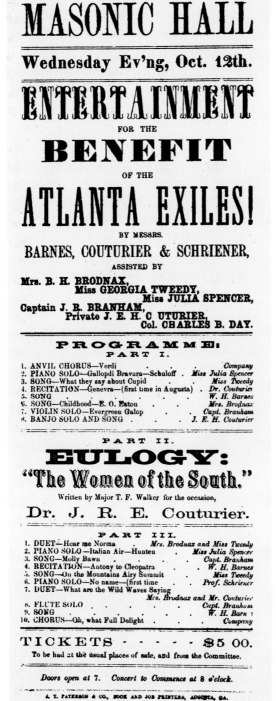

MASONIC HALL

Wednesday Ev'ng, Oct. 12th.

ENTERTAINMENT

FOR THE

BENEFIT

OF THE

ATLANTA EXILES!

BY MESSRS.

BARNES, COUTURIER & SCHRIENER,

ASSISTED BY

Mrs. B. H. BRODNAX,
Miss GEORGIA TWEEDY,
Miss JULIA SPENCER,
Captain J. R. BRANHAM,
Private J. E. H. COUTURIER,
Col. CHARLES B. DAY.

PROGRAMME:

PART I.

1. ANVIL CHORUS—Verdi . . . . *Company*
2. PIANO SOLO—Gallopdi Bravura—Schuloff . *Miss Julia Spencer*
3. SONG—What they say about Cupid . . *Miss Tweedy*
4. RECITATION—Genevra—(first time in Augusta) . *Dr. Couturier*
5. SONG . . . . . . *W. H. Barnes*
6. SONG—Childhood—E. O. Eaton . . *Mrs. Brodnax*
7. VIOLIN SOLO—Evergreen Galop . . *Capt. Branham*
8. BANJO SOLO AND SONG . . . *J. E. H. Couturier*

PART II.

EULOGY:

"The Women of the South."

Written by Major T. F. Walker for the occasion,

Dr. J. R. E. Couturier.

PART III.

1. DUET—Hear me Norma . *Mrs. Brodnax and Miss Tweedy*
2. PIANO SOLO—Italian Air—Hunten . *Miss Julia Spencer*
3. SONG—Molly Bawn . . . . *Capt. Branham*
4. RECITATION—Antony to Cleopatra . *W. H. Barnes*
5. SONG—On the Mountains Airy Summit . *Miss Tweedy*
6. PIANO SOLO—No name—(first time . *Prof. Schriener*
7. DUET—What are the Wild Waves Saying
. *Mrs. Brodnax and Mr. Couturier*
8. FLUTE SOLO . . . . *Capt. Branham*
9. SONG . . . . . . *W. H. Barnes*
10. CHORUS—Oh, what Full Delight . . *Company*

TICKETS - - - - - $5 00.

To be had at the usual places of sale, and from the Committee.

Doors open at 7.   Concert to Commence at 8 o'clock.

J. T. PATERSON & CO., BOOK AND JOB PRINTERS, AUGUSTA, GA.

This handbill, touting an evening of music and dramatic readings, was circulated among the citizens of Augusta, Georgia, in the early weeks of October 1864. The proceeds of the event were used to aid the homeless evacuees of Atlanta.

Hood's army was stirring and seemed about to embark on a campaign of its own. Like his adversary, Hood had been intently considering his next move. He desperately needed to damage the Federal army and regain the esteem he had lost by giving up Atlanta. Many Confederates were arguing that Hood should be cashiered, not only for having been maneuvered out of the city, but also for having lost 21,000 killed and wounded in his ill-considered attempts to drive off Sherman's larger army. These losses made it impossible for Hood to tackle Sherman head on again. He would have to find another way to confound his enemy, strike a blow for the Confederacy and recoup his own reputation.

Hood's solution was a daring one: to reverse directions, marching his troops back to the northwest toward Chattanooga and Nashville. That way he could tear up the railroad to Atlanta, choking off Sherman's supplies and gobbling up the detachments Sherman had left behind to guard his life line. This move, as Hood saw it, would force Sherman to backtrack and eventually to abandon Atlanta. There was, Hood later wrote, "but one plan to be adopted: by maneuvers to draw Sherman back into the mountains, then beat him in battle, and at least regain our lost territory." If successful, Hood might be able to invade Tennessee, taking Nashville, and then perhaps continue his advance and reenter Kentucky. Executed with enough dash, such a campaign might defeat the Federal forces in the west and reverse the tide of the entire War.

Despite his recent defeats, such visions of martial derring-do came easily to Hood. He had gained fame as a recklessly bold commander under Robert E. Lee during the fighting in Virginia. At Gaines's Mill and Second Bull Run he had led crucial attacks; at Antietam he had saved General Lee from catastrophe. But he had paid a terrible price: At Gettysburg a shell had ripped his left arm from hand to biceps, rendering it useless; at Chickamauga a bullet in his thigh had led to the amputation of his leg near the hip.

Hood had been lionized for his heroism, and at 33 he had become the youngest full general in the Confederate Army. His swift rise to fame and rank had fed his ambition, but at the same time his wounds reminded him of his own mortality. And he had fallen in love, with a woman whose parents disapproved of the match, leaving Hood uncertain and often distraught.

In this condition — heartsore, buffeted by ambition, walking on crutches and riding strapped to his saddle, sometimes befuddled by the opiate, laudanum, that he took to numb his almost-constant pain — Hood had found himself heading the Army of Tennessee. Never known for prudence, he seemed more volatile than ever now that he held the command of an entire army. On September 8 Hood demanded that Confederate President Jefferson Davis remove the army's most experienced corps commander, Lieutenant General William Hardee, whom Hood dis-

liked and blamed for the debacles around Atlanta. Davis probably regretted this — he respected Hardee's military skill and liked the man for his apolitical nature. But since he was not willing to fire Hood, Davis reluctantly posted Hardee to Charleston to take charge of the Department of South Carolina, Georgia and Florida.

Thus a personal animus cost Hood the services of one of the Confederacy's most effective officers. Trying to make up for Hardee's departure, Davis soon placed General P.G.T. Beauregard in overall charge of the Military Division of the West, with the hope that the older and more experienced professional could advise Hood and perhaps keep him out of trouble.

The loss of Hardee did little to encourage the officers and men of the Army of Tennessee, many of whom despised Hood for sacrificing so many lives in the attacks on Sherman around Atlanta. Desertion became a chronic problem. To make matters worse, Hood's troops were bone-tired and lacked supplies and equipment. Forced to abandon Atlanta in a rush, they had burned munitions laboriously collected from all over the Confederacy. The men were also short of other basics — shoes, clothes, weapons. Even food was scarce because Georgia farmers had be-

come increasingly reluctant to sell their produce in exchange for the inflated Confederate paper currency.

Despite his swarming troubles, Hood was determined to go on the offensive. He could not stand still and watch his army erode as more and more dispirited men decamped. He was sure that an offensive would be a tonic for his soldiers, infusing them with renewed fighting spirit. Even the lack of reinforcements failed to daunt him. On September 21 he shifted his army 20 miles west of Lovejoy's Station to Palmetto, and the next day he informed Richmond that he had decided on an offensive. "Sherman is weaker now than he will be in the future," Hood wired, "and I as strong as I can expect to be." The move to Palmetto placed his troops southwest of Atlanta and in an excellent position to strike due north at Sherman's communications. On September 29, Hood led his troops across the Chattahoochee River. He was launched on a campaign that would have the most fateful effect on the course of the entire conflict.

Hood headed north in a steady march, covering 12 to 18 miles a day. On October 1 his cavalry hit the Western & Atlantic Railroad — the stretch of Sherman's life line between Chattanooga and Atlanta — and tore up some track. This was merely a pinprick. More serious damage was done a couple of days later when one of the Confederate infantry corps, commanded by Lieutenant General Alexander P. Stewart, appeared in force before the outposts guarding the railroad at Acworth and at Big Shanty. Stewart's men captured most of the Federal troops at both garrisons and ripped up 15 miles of tracks and ties.

Sherman had concluded by October 2 that Hood and his entire army were on the move and headed back up the Union's supply line. Sherman had been forewarned that this might be Hood's plan by Federal spies and by newspaper accounts of an imprudent speech delivered by Jefferson Davis in which the Confederate President had all but outlined Hood's projected campaign. Sherman had already sent General Thomas steaming northward by train all the way to Nashville, followed by two divisions that had been ordered to protect Chattanooga. Part of Thomas' mission was to subdue the Confederate cavalry commander, Nathan Bedford Forrest, whose troopers had been on a lengthy and destructive raid through middle Tennessee. But clearly Thomas had not had the time — nor as yet did he have the men — to

A series of photographs taken from a seminary steeple soon after the capture of Atlanta on September 2, 1864, provides a rare panoramic view of the city under Sherman's occupation. On the horizon at center are Atlanta's train station and business district. Many of these buildings would be destroyed when Sherman abandoned the city in November.

mount a defense against both Forrest's riders and Hood's approaching infantrymen. Sherman himself would have to move back toward Chattanooga to try to prevent Hood from tearing up the Federal life line and advancing into Tennessee.

Shelving his march to Savannah, Sherman moved fast. He dispatched a division commanded by Brigadier General John M. Corse to defend the town of Rome, 50 miles northwest of Atlanta, should the Confederates veer in that direction. Then on October 3, leaving Major General Henry Slocum and the 12,000 men of XX Corps to guard Atlanta, Sherman started the bulk of his army, five corps totaling about 55,000 troops, for Marietta, 15 miles to the north.

Sherman was in a foul humor. He was being forced to draw back over the same ground, just as Hood had planned. Riding near the front of his long column as usual, nervously snapping the ash from his cigars, Sherman crossed the Chattahoochee River and headed his forces into the Georgia hills.

On October 4, as Federal advance units neared Kennesaw Mountain, Sherman learned that part of Hood's force, about 2,000 men under Major General Samuel French, was marching up the railroad for Allatoona Pass, where a small Union garrison stood guard over some of Sherman's largest supply warehouses. At Allatoona Pass the previous spring, General Joseph Johnston, Hood's predecessor, had skillfully delayed Sherman's original advance. Now it was the Federals' turn to defend the pass. Since French's Confederate force was more than large enough to smash the garrison holding the pass, Sherman sent a message to Corse at Rome, ordering him to reinforce Allatoona with all possible haste.

Corse, a flamboyant 29-year-old of striking courage, had spent two years at West Point before quitting the military academy to study law in Iowa and then had joined the Federal Army when the War began. Sherman admired Corse despite the young Iowan's penchant for boisterous profanity and his pronounced although perhaps unconscious knack for self-dramatization.

On receiving Sherman's signaled order, Corse managed to get 1,054 of his men aboard 20 commandeered railroad cars. He then hurried south on the Western & Atlantic to Allatoona, arriving about one in the morning on October 5. Corse immediately sent the train back to Rome to pick up the

Confederate General John Bell Hood, who succeeded Joseph Johnston as commander of the Army of Tennessee, served in California with the United States Army before the War. In San Francisco in 1855, Hood met William T. Sherman, then a banker, and was struck by the "piercing eye and nervous impulsive temperament" of the man who was to become his adversary.

General Sherman leans against the breech of a 20-pounder Parrott gun at a Union fort in Atlanta, during the Federal occupation of the city. The fort was part of Sherman's effort to contract the city's lines of defense, a project overseen by his chief engineer, Captain Orlando Poe (*fourth from left*).

remaining troops under his command, but the locomotive derailed, cutting off further Federal reinforcements.

At Allatoona, Corse joined Lieutenant Colonel John Tourtellotte and his 890-man garrison. The two officers swiftly deployed their troops to meet an attack. At the south end of the pass, the troops manned a complex of rifle pits and trenches dug atop a crooked ridge that was bisected by a 60-foot-deep cut, through which ran the railroad. Most elaborate of the works were two redoubts, about 75 feet in diameter, which were on opposite sides of the railroad cut. Corse, in overall command, took up his position in the redoubt to the west while Colonel Tourtellotte took charge of the fort to the east of the tracks.

By sunrise Corse and Tourtellotte had their men in position — and none too soon. At 7:30, Major John D. Myrick, who was commanding the Confederate artillery, ordered his 12 guns to open fire on the Federal forts. As a hail of shell and solid shot began raining on the redoubts, Confederate skirmishers started to close in on the Federal outposts. Soon a steady crackle of rifle fire was echoing through the ravines and hills that surrounded the Federal position.

While the skirmishers pressed forward, General French dispatched one of his brigades, Mississippians under Brigadier General Claudius W. Sears, on a sweep to the northeast to get behind the redoubts. With little opposition, Sears's troops cut the railroad and telegraph lines north of Allatoona Pass, leaving Corse without communications. By 8:30 a.m. French had placed his other two brigades, Brigadier General William H. Young's Texas brigade and Brigadier General Francis M. Cockrell's Missourians, in position to the west of the pass. With the Federals effectively surrounded, French sent Corse a peremptory ultimatum under a flag of truce. To avoid a "needless effusion of blood," French's message read, Corse was to surrender unconditionally — and he was to do so within five minutes.

Union General John M. Corse (below) arrived with troops to bolster the garrison at Allatoona, Georgia, only hours before Confederate General Samuel G. French (bottom) attacked on October 5, 1864. Allatoona was an important supply depot and its loss, one Federal soldier remarked, would have meant "a disastrous ending to a hitherto successful campaign."

The Union's General Corse, seen in the background against a cloud of smoke with his sword held high, leads his troops out from behind their breastworks at Allatoona to repulse Confederate attackers. At far right, a Federal signal officer with a flag sends news of the battle to General Sherman's post 14 miles away on Kennesaw Mountain.

Corse instantly dashed off a polite refusal. "Your communication demanding surrender of my command I acknowledge receipt of, and respectfully reply that we are prepared for the 'needless effusion of blood' whenever it is agreeable to you. I am, very respectfully, your obedient servant."

Corse now hurried about his embattled works, readying his troops for the impending attack. "I had hardly issued the incipient orders," he recalled, "when the storm broke in all its fury." West of the railroad cut, the men of the 39th Iowa and the 7th Illinois, defending rifle pits and trenches, were the first to feel the weight of the Confederate attack. General Young's Texas brigade struck first and was held off by the Illinois troops, who used their Henry repeating rifles to deadly effect. But then Sears's Mississippians hit "like a wintry blast from the North," recalled a Federal cavalry officer named Mortimer Flint, forcing the Federals to fall back on the west redoubt. Colonel Richard Rowett, commander of the 7th Illinois, was wounded, and Colonel James Redfield of the 39th Iowa, already hit three times, was killed by a bullet through the heart. Another Illinois regiment, the 93rd, fell back rapidly, losing its colors but managing to beat the Confederates in a race for the redoubt's protecting ditch.

As the fight at Allatoona Pass was heating up, General Sherman rode onto Kennesaw Mountain, across a broad valley to the south 14 miles away. As Sherman recalled in his memoirs, he could "plainly see the smoke of battle about Allatoona, and hear the faint reverberation of the cannon." The signal officer on Kennesaw had been trying vainly since daylight to obtain an answer to his wig-wagged messages, but then while Sherman was with him he "caught a faint glimpse of the tell-tale flag through an embrasure, and after much time he had made out these letters — 'C,' 'R,' 'S,' 'E,' 'H,' 'E,' 'R.' " Sherman is said to have pondered the message a moment and then to have shouted, "I understand it! Corse is there all right. He'll hold out. I know the man!"

Sherman's conviction that Corse would be able to hold Allatoona seemed for a time to be wishful thinking. All along the western segment of the Federal line the Confederates were pressing in for the kill, despite heavy fire from the embattled strong point. Colonel William H. Clark of the 46th Mississippi actually reached the ditch that ran outside the Federal redoubt, waving the regimental flag and urging his men on in their attack until he was shot down.

Corse quickly decided he needed reinforcements. Soon the men of the 12th and 50th Illinois were dashing across the fire-swept railroad cut from Tourtellotte's redoubt, which was under less vigorous attack. The two Illinois regiments crowded into the west redoubt's ditch with the Federal troops already fighting there. They arrived just in time to beat back an attack by the 14th Texas Cavalry (Dismounted), whose men were at a disadvantage in hand-to-hand combat because, being horsemen originally, they had never been issued bayonets. The Texans fell back, taking refuge in some buildings only 40 yards from the redoubt. From windows in the upper stories, they poured rifle fire directly into the fort, picking off many defenders, until they were blasted out by point-blank artillery fire.

French's troops continued to mount sporadic assaults, working their way closer and closer to the western redoubt. They were

These two views of Kennesaw Mountain, where General Sherman anxiously awaited news from Allatoona on October 5, show its signal post (*top*) and the vista from a high outlook (*bottom*). Known as "the twin mountain," Kennesaw was the formidable range that Sherman captured in June after a costly battle with the forces of General Joseph Johnston. A Federal soldier called Kennesaw "the most perfect natural fortification Sherman's army ever encountered."

The Signal Post on Kinesaw Mt, Ga.
Talking to Alatoona, Oct 6th 1864

able to take "advantage of the rough ground surrounding the fort," Corse later wrote in a report, "filling every hole and trench, seeking shelter behind every stump and log that lay within musket range."

A Confederate bullet finally found Corse. The ball grazed the side of the Federal commander's face, severing a vein, nicking an ear and knocking him out cold. Ammunition was running low, and Corse's second-in-command ordered the men to conserve what remained. The cries of "Cease firing!" running down the line penetrated Corse's stupor and he bounded up, cursing angrily. "No surrender, hold Allatoona!" shouted the still-befuddled commander, reopening his wound in the process so that blood rushed down his face.

Corse then turned to his artillerymen. They reported that their supplies of canister were nearly exhausted. An officer immediately volunteered to cross the railroad cut and secure a fresh supply from Tourtellotte's redoubt. Noticing a narrow footbridge, he dashed across, reached the second fort and gathered up as many canister rounds as he could carry. He then staggered back across the bridge, shells and bullets whistling past his ears.

Artillerymen of the 12th Wisconsin Battery swiftly put the ammunition to use. One of their three guns, stationed outside the redoubt, had been overrun by the Confederates, but now the cannon was back in Federal hands. It had been recovered by an already-wounded artillery sergeant who, calling for volunteers to help, had rushed outside the fort and secured the prize, sustaining several more wounds. "A bloodier man was never seen," recalled a Federal engineer, Major William Ludlow, "but he kept at his work until a musket ball passed though his neck and he dropped dead."

By four in the afternoon, General French was in trouble. His regiments had become so disorganized that he could no longer hope to storm the Federal redoubts. In addition, he had received information — incorrect as it turned out — that a large Federal force was threatening to cut him off from the main Confederate army about 20 miles to the southwest around Dallas. French had little choice as he saw it but to withdraw. He soon pulled out to the southwest to rejoin Hood, leaving behind 799 men killed, wounded and captured — and forfeiting a million rations of hardtack that he had hoped to scoop up from Allatoona's warehouses.

The next day Corse counted his casualties, 706 in all, and sent Sherman a characteristically jubilant and dramatic message: "I am short a cheekbone and an ear, but am able to whip all hell yet!" A few days later Sherman saw his flamboyant general. Corse was wearing a bandage on his cheek, but there was little sign of damage to the ear that he claimed to have lost. Sherman was pleased with Corse, who had performed a valuable service for his chief by saving Allatoona from the Confederates. Had Corse lost the important supply base, Grant and the high command in Washington might well have dashed Sherman's hopes for the march to the sea. Now Sherman laughed at the sight of his officer. "Corse," he exclaimed, "they came damned near missing you, didn't they?"

The Battle of Allatoona gave rise to one of the War's imperishable sayings. At some point during the fighting, the signal officer on Kennesaw Mountain evidently sent an encouraging message to Corse and his defenders: "General Sherman says hold fast;

A Union supply train with General Sherman's forces makes slow progress up a treacherous rain-slickened mountain path during the pursuit of Hood's Confederate army into Alabama in October 1864. In the foreground, soldiers using poles attempt to pry a wagon out of the mud.

we are coming.'' Journalists seized on the incident, reporting that Sherman had signaled, ''Hold the fort; I am coming.'' In this altered form the message captured the popular imagination of the North, making the defense of the supply depot more famous than other battles of far greater significance. A

well-known evangelist of the time, Philip Paul Bliss, soon made the words the theme of a revival hymn titled ''Hold the Fort.'' Bliss's hymn swept the country and embedded the phrase in the language.

The day after the fighting ended at Allatoona, October 6, Samuel French and his

troops rejoined the main Confederate army. Hood was still near Dallas, but he was ready to move again and soon did so, marching swiftly to the northwest, aiming to outpace Sherman. His strategy was to cross the Coosa River west of Rome; then he would either draw Sherman into battle somewhere near the Alabama line or head for the Western & Atlantic tracks at Resaca about 40 miles south of Chattanooga, hoping for a decisive fight there.

Hood moved so quickly that Sherman's patrols lost contact with the Confederates, who seemed to have suddenly vanished. Briefly Sherman feared his adversary was circling back for a strike against Atlanta, and he wired General Slocum to be alert. Then word came that the Confederate column was again moving northward, still farther into the Georgia hills.

Sherman had fought through this inhospitable country the summer before, and he did not relish having to do so again. He grumbled bitterly in a letter to Corse that Hood was too unpredictable: "I cannot guess his movements as I could those of Johnston, who was a sensible man and only did sensible things." Still, he felt constrained for the moment to continue to move farther north himself, staying on the defensive, reacting instead of acting, trailing behind his adversary like a child in tow.

While Sherman complained, Hood decided on his next move. "The effect of our operations so far surpassed my expectations," he wrote later, that rather than trying to draw Sherman into Alabama, he would take the bolder route, advancing directly toward Resaca and Chattanooga, destroying the rails as he went. Sherman, Hood reckoned, would continue to follow, dropping off troops to

General P.G.T. Beauregard, who took command of the Confederacy's newly created Military Division of the West on October 17, 1864, was dissatisfied with this largely administrative appointment. "My greatest desire has always been to command a good army in the field," he remarked before accepting the post. "Will I never be gratified?"

repair and protect the railroad as he went and thus weakening his army. Then, somewhere in the broken country near the Tennessee border, Hood's men would be waiting. "It was my fixed purpose to attack Sherman," Hood explained, "as soon as I succeeded in these maneuvers."

If Hood was confident of success, General Beauregard, the newly appointed commander of the Western Theater, was not. Beauregard caught up with Hood on October 9 at Cave Spring, a north Georgia spa in happier times, to discuss what Hood had in mind. As Beauregard listened, his heart sank. Hood was about to undertake a complex and risky movement without sufficient planning, Beauregard concluded, and with many things "left to further determination and even luck." Nevertheless, Beauregard decided not to interfere. He had not formally assumed his new command, and an argument with Hood so early seemed undesirable. He therefore acquiesced to Hood's plan and went off to Jacksonville, Alabama, to set up his new headquarters.

Undeterred by Beauregard's doubts, General Hood moved northeast with a force that overwhelmed the small Federal garrisons along the railroad. Most of these outposts surrendered readily, but when Hood got to Resaca on October 12 he came up against another Federal officer who, like John Corse at Allatoona, refused to be intimidated. This was Colonel Clark R. Wever of the 17th Iowa, who was acting as commanding officer of a brigade from XV Corps garrisoned at Resaca. Wever, hearing that a strong enemy force was approaching, drew in detachments that were scattered along the rail line nearby, deepened old rifle pits, dug new ones and set up palisades around his works. Satisfied that his defenses were formidable, he awaited Hood's assault.

Hood had his skirmish line attack briefly, then drew his troops close to the Federal breastworks and sent in a menacing note, calling on Wever and his small garrison to throw down their arms. "I demand immediate and unconditional surrender of the post and garrison under your command," Hood wrote. He added, "If the place is carried by assault, no prisoners will be taken."

Wever answered with dignity that he was surprised by Hood's raw threat. Then he boldly challenged Hood to attack. "In my opinion I can hold this post. If you want it, come and take it."

As he considered Wever's intransigence, Hood had second thoughts about attacking. It might take some time to overcome the defiant colonel and his garrison. Sherman was past Rome by now and no doubt closing rapidly. Hood concluded that taking Resaca was not worth the effort. Leaving part of his force confronting Resaca, he continued north, marching 15 miles to Dalton, where the garrison capitulated after a brief fight, and to Tunnel Hill, where the Federal defenders surrendered on demand.

Hood's two-week campaign had been so far a considerable achievement. Tunnel Hill was where Sherman had begun his triumphant march to Atlanta early the previous May. Now Hood had forced him and much of his army to retrace their steps through the fogs and rains of autumn. And the Federals had nothing to show for all their footsore reverse marching because they had not managed to corner the Confederates and force a fight.

Hood's successes, nevertheless, rang a bit hollow. General Slocum still held Atlanta unthreatened. The broken rail lines could be repaired, and both Slocum and Sherman had ample supplies to last until the railroad was fully operational again. To consolidate his gains, Hood knew that he would have to tempt Sherman into a pitched battle and then defeat him. A Confederate victory would break Sherman's grip on Atlanta and northern Georgia, restore confidence throughout the Confederacy — and open the way for further advances into Tennessee and even beyond.

It soon appeared that the two commanders were going to get the fight they both wanted. Hood consolidated his forces near Resaca and then withdrew northwestward about 15 miles through Snake Creek Gap, blocking the gap behind him with felled timber. Major General Oliver Howard's Army of the

The home at left belonged to Charles Henry Smith (*above*), who wrote humorous wartime sketches under the name Bill Arp. Smith's place was occupied in May of 1864 by Union General William Vandever, who is shown third from left (*seated*) with members of his staff.

The Refugee Humorist

"If Mr. Shakspeer wer korrekt when he writ that 'sweet are the juices of adversity,' then it are reasunable to supose that me and my foaks must hav sum sweetnin to spar." So wrote the journalist Charles Henry Smith — in the voice of his literary creation, Bill Arp — when, in May of 1864, Smith and his family were forced by Federal troops to abandon their home in Rome, Georgia. While a refugee, Smith continued to contribute weekly letters from Bill Arp to the Atlanta *Constitution* as he had done since the beginning of the War. These letters, written in the semiliterate dialect favored by many 19th Century American humorists, mingled the "sweet and pashent sadness" of the beleaguered South with a good-humored tolerance of the hardships of war. "I joined the army and succeeded in killing about as many of them as they of me," Smith once remarked, demonstrating the wry wit that won him the title of "the best loved man in all the Southland."

"In the dark days," the Savannah *Press* once said of Smith, "he kept Southern hearts from breaking." Bill Arp himself expressed a similar sentiment about the songs and jokes that passed among refugees on the road. "These things," he wrote, "together with the komik events that okkured by the way, wer the safety valves that saved the poor hart from bustin." After the War, Smith's writings were collected and were published as a book. The title page is at right, along with illustrations and excerpts from the volume.

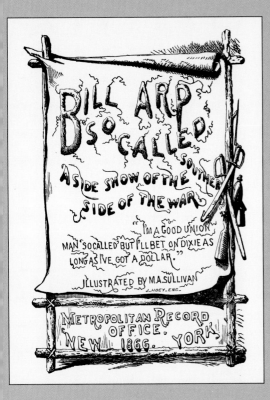

"*Then wer xhibited to our afflikted gaze a hiway krowded with waggins and teems, kattle and hogs, niggers and dogs, wimmen and childern, all movin in disheveld haist to parts unknown . . . Everybody was kontinualy lookin behind and drivin befo — everybody wanted to kno everything, and nobody knu nothin.*"

'*It wer in the ded of winter, thru snow and thru sleet, over kreeks without bridges and bridges without floors, thru a deserted and deserlate land wher no rooster was left to krow, no pig to squeel, no dog to bark, wher the rooins of happy hoams adorned the way, and ghostly chimniz stood up like Sherman's sentinels a gardin the rooins he had made.*"

31

Tennessee was in hot pursuit. "My command," Howard wrote, "threw the gap obstructions to the right and left and camped close up to Hood's rear guard." When Sherman came to Howard's position on October 17, he was delighted to find that Hood's main force was near a town named La Fayette, "a place I hoped to catch him and force him to battle."

Hood, full of enthusiasm, called his officers together for a council of war — and found them unanimously opposed to giving battle. Hood was astonished. He argued that the troops, after a "forward movement of 100 miles," were full of "confidence, enthusiasm, and hope of victory." His officers admitted that the condition of the men was much improved, but not so much that they could take on Sherman's numbers with any hope of success.

Hood chose not to fly in the face of unanimous opinion. He knew that he had no hope for success in a battle that his officers expected to lose. So he broke camp and moved southwestward, his army retreating down the rough Chattooga River Valley and across the Alabama line toward Gaylesville and Gadsden. Hood was disappointed — and confirmed in his opinion that many of his officers had lost their nerve.

Sherman, also disappointed at having been cheated of the opportunity to deal with Hood once and for all, followed by leisurely stages. He was certain now that Hood had "no intention to meet us in open battle, and the lightness and celerity of his army convinced me that I could not possibly catch him on a stern chase." What was more, he had lost all interest in trying. "Hood can turn and twist like a fox," he wrote General Thomas, "and wear out my army in pursuit." When the Federal column arrived in Gaylesville, Sherman stopped. By that time Hood and his Confederates had reached Gadsden, 30 miles farther into Alabama.

It was not in Hood's nature, however, to keep on retreating. Whatever he thought of his subordinate officers, he was sure that his soldiers could and would fight if given an inspiring objective. Hood had evidently decided what that objective would be before retreating from La Fayette. He would regroup at Gadsden, march north to Guntersville, cross the Tennessee River there and head for Chattanooga. Before Sherman could react, he would catch George Thomas by surprise, smashing the scattered Federal detachments en route.

Once in Tennessee, Hood's men would fatten on the enemy's food stores, reequip themselves with new shoes and clothes from Federal warehouses and rearm themselves from Federal arsenals. Like other Confederate generals before him, Hood envisioned that Confederate sympathizers in the state would flock to join his army. He thought that even more recruits would enlist when his renewed army forged on into Kentucky. If Sherman continued his pursuit, Hood would meet and defeat him. Otherwise, Hood would march to the Ohio River, or perhaps he would turn eastward, cross the Cumberland Mountains and join forces with Robert E. Lee in Virginia. There his army and Lee's would catch Grant's army in a vise, destroying it and winning the War.

It was a dreamy plan based on unrealistic assumptions, but it seems to have brought the beleaguered, pain-racked Hood a great deal of pleasure. The same could not be said for General Beauregard. Hearing to his astonishment that Hood's army was at Gads-

Confederate Private Reuben Nations of the 12th Louisiana, shown here at the start of the War, took part in a reconnaissance of Sherman's forces at Decatur, Alabama, on October 28, 1864. Advancing to determine the strength of the Federal garrison, Nations was struck by a shell that shattered his legs below the knee. Both legs had to be amputated.

den rather than engaged to the north at the Tennessee border as planned, Beauregard hurried from his Jacksonville headquarters to Gadsden for another conference. He was dumfounded when Hood announced his new strategy for invasion — all the more so because Hood had not consulted him beforehand about the wildly ambitious scheme.

Beauregard was a skilled officer and well aware of the difficulty of moving large numbers of men over great distances; it was doubtless clear to him that the intricacy of the proposed moves surpassed Hood's experience and probably his ability as well. But Beauregard neither objected nor insisted on assuming command, which was his prerogative. He knew they had no time for a command squabble. And should they come to a test of wills, Beauregard had no reason to suppose that Jefferson Davis would support

him against Hood. Besides, Beauregard had no better plan to offer.

So, with a firm admonishment that speed was crucial if the Confederates were to surprise Thomas, Beauregard sent Hood off. Hood's soldiers went wild when definite word came that they were going to Tennessee — home for a number of them. The camp rang with the high-pitched Rebel yell, a most welcome sound to Hood, who was more used to his men's complaints.

As the army marched off, Beauregard stayed behind in Gadsden tending to chores that Hood had overlooked. In a characteristic lapse, Hood had forgotten to take up his pontoon bridge, which still lay across the Coosa River. Beauregard got the pontoons loaded on their carriages and sent them along after Hood; then he awaited news of the crossing at Guntersville.

Hood did not bother to inform Beauregard, but word drifted in: The Federal presence at Guntersville was too strong and Hood was going on to Decatur, about 45 miles farther west. There were Federals at Decatur as well, however, and the river was too high; Hood's men would march another 20 miles to Courtland. At Courtland the crossing looked difficult and Hood decided to move on once more, to Tuscumbia. The whole idea of speed, on which everything depended, seemed to have been forgotten.

Hood and his army were in the Decatur area before Sherman learned that the Confederates had left Gadsden. Now Hood's designs on Tennessee were obvious — and Sherman was delighted. "Damn him!" Sherman cried. "If he will go to the Ohio River, I'll give him rations." Let him go north, he added, "my business is down south."

Sherman had already sent Major General

33

David S. Stanley and his IV Corps — 15,000 men — to Tennessee with orders to be alert for some such move on the part of Hood. Now Sherman detached from his army at Gaylesville the 12,000-man XXIII Corps under Major General John Schofield, who would assume command of the entire force of 27,000. Schofield would report to George Thomas in Nashville. So would Major General Andrew J. Smith, who had been ordered to move his corps of about 13,000 from Missouri to Tennessee. With the troops already garrisoned in Chattanooga and stationed at other strategic points, Thomas would have more than 70,000 men to oppose Hood's invading army — ample forces, Sherman felt, for Thomas to hold Tennessee.

Having issued these orders, Sherman next stepped up his campaign to convince Grant, President Lincoln and other officials that his march to the sea was a judicious idea attended by far fewer risks than the many that appeared to more cautious eyes. "Instead of being on the defensive," Sherman had wired Grant a few days earlier, "I would be on the offensive." At the moment, Sherman pointed out, Hood was dictating Federal strategy in the west. It was necessary to again wrest the initiative from the Confederates. Besides, he added, Thomas could parry any punch that Hood might manage to throw.

The Union high command was less confident on both counts — that Sherman could get through to the sea unscathed and that Thomas could contain Hood. At just this crucial moment in late October, Nathan Bedford Forrest again rode out of the woods with his wild cavalrymen to destroy Federal shipping on the Tennessee River and to threaten the important supply depot at the river town of Johnsonville — where he subsequently battered the Federal garrison and set fire to large quantities of stores.

Forrest's sudden eruption immediately prompted cautioning measures from the high command, and a dispatch from Grant was delivered to Sherman on November 1 that opened with a question and closed with an order. "Do you not think it advisable, now that Hood has gone so far north, to entirely ruin him before starting on your proposed campaign?" After some rumination, the message ended, "If you can see a chance of destroying Hood's army, attend to that first and make your other move secondary."

Sherman impatiently responded the next day. "If I could hope to overhaul Hood," he wired, "I would turn against him with my whole force." But that was a vain hope. "No single army can catch Hood," Sherman continued. "General Thomas will have a force strong enough to prevent his reaching any country in which we have an interest." If he were to chase Hood any farther, Sherman went on to say, "the whole effect of my campaign will be lost." It was patently clear to him, the general concluded, "that the best results will follow my contemplated movement through Georgia."

Sherman's response finally persuaded Grant. "Go on as you propose," he wrote. But having changed his mind, Grant had a new problem to solve. He had argued so effectively against Sherman's scheme that President Lincoln was now dead set against it. Grant would have to alter Lincoln's thinking, too. Now he sent a message to the President that "Sherman's proposition is the best that can be adopted." His subordinate's scheme was admittedly risky, but Sherman and his army would be "hard to corner or capture." No other Union general had

Union drovers herd cattle eastward across the Coosa River in Alabama while a division of Sherman's Army of the Tennessee crosses a pontoon bridge in the middle distance. The crossing occurred in early November 1864, after Sherman had broken off his pursuit of John Bell Hood and was returning to Atlanta to undertake the march to the Atlantic Coast.

proved himself such a master of maneuver, Grant argued. If Sherman thought that he could march from Atlanta to the sea, then he almost certainly could.

The President was swiftly persuaded. Having at last found a pair of generals who would and could both move and fight, Lincoln was inclined to give these officers a free rein. "Whatever results, you have the confidence and support of the Government," wired Major General Henry Halleck, Army Chief of Staff, from Washington.

With permission to launch his march to the sea, Sherman immediately began moving his army back toward Atlanta. At last he had regained the initiative. By November 14 Sherman himself was in Atlanta. On the 15th he was prepared to move.

But Hood was getting ready to resume the offensive as well — and one of the strangest scenes in the history of warfare was about to unfold. Two major armies that had been locked in combat and maneuver for months now prepared to march in opposite directions, each with an objective that had nothing to do with the other.

The Men Who Marched to the Sea

If, as General Sherman once wrote, there is a "soul to an army as well as to the individual man," then the troops that marched to the sea may be said to have had four souls — one for each of the army's distinct corps of infantry. Each of the four corps, plus a contingent of cavalry, was filled with battle-hardened veterans, who had passed through a rigorous weeding-out process at the outset of the march that left behind only the young and fit — the "little devils," as Sherman once called them.

XIV Corps was known for its wide range of battle experience as well as for the free-wheeling style that characterized western troops. Sometimes the casual air of the corps bordered on insubordination — as it did when soldiers of the 17th Ohio *(far right)* took it upon themselves to groom their commander's prized gray stallion by shaving its tail. But such was the close-knit nature of the corps that no one would step forward to identify the culprits, despite the offer of a $500 reward.

Often the unfettered ways of XIV Corps caused friction with the Easterners of XX Corps, with whom they marched, but beneath the regional differences lay a unity of purpose symbolized by General Sherman's headquarters flag *(right, bottom)*, which blended elements of the four individual corps flags. A soldier on the march put it simply: Asked to which corps he belonged, he indignantly replied, "Corps? What do you mean, 'corps?' I belong to General Sherman's army."

MEN OF THE 5TH OHIO CAVALRY

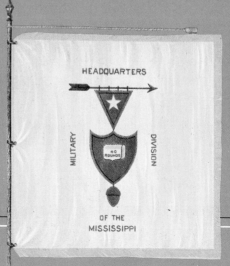

SHERMAN'S HEADQUARTERS FLAG

XIV CORPS HEADQUARTERS FLAG

MEN OF THE 17TH OHIO

CAPTAIN JAMES LADD
OF THE 113TH OHIO

OFFICERS AND NCOs
OF THE 86TH ILLINOIS

FORTY ROUNDS
US

The Weary Campaigners

The men of XV Corps, another western outfit, had been worn down by extended campaigning and a recurring lack of supplies. Sergeant John Risedorph of the 4th Minnesota *(far right, bottom)* began the march barefoot; but with a determination characteristic of his corps he noted in his diary, "I have thought I could not go another step, but some irresistible influence urges me along." Captain George Pepper, the chaplain of the 80th Ohio *(above, seated farthest right)*, set out from Atlanta with only "a towel, a cracker, a Testament, and a late Southern paper, announcing Sherman's retreat from Hood." In the face of these hardships, the men of XV Corps shared fully in the proud spirit of the campaign — a feeling captured by Captain Neal Neff of the 54th Ohio *(right, holding hat)*, who described the march in a poem: "Those columns long and strong, in blue, To freedom and the Union true, Did again their forward march pursue, O'er hill and rill and plain."

UNKNOWN PRIVATE, 100TH INDIANA

CAPTAIN NEAL NEFF, 54TH OHIO

OFFICERS OF THE 80TH OHIO,
2ND BRIGADE, 3RD DIVISION

SERGEANT JOHN RISEDORPH,
4TH MINNESOTA

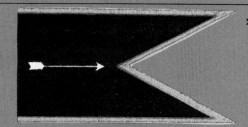

An Ability to Adapt

The troops of XVII Corps had a long and successful battle record of which they were very proud. Already used to the deprivations of war, the westerners of the corps adapted easily to the vicissitudes of the march to the sea. Cut off from their regular sources of supply, the men foraged with a will and made do with what they had; their spirits remained high. F. Y. Hedley, adjutant of the 32nd Illinois, wrote of "toothsome" meals of confiscated pork or beef broiled at the end of a ramrod and of treasured decks of cards so worn from use that the markings could no longer be distinguished. The competition for food was intense, and sometimes arguments arose over its possession. Such disputes, remembered 18-year-old Captain Charles Belknap, were all that threatened to disrupt the "brotherly love" in his corps.

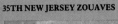
35TH NEW JERSEY ZOUAVES

TWO OFFICERS, 45TH ILLINOIS

MAJOR H. WILSON & CAPTAIN W. NEAL, 20TH OHIO

OFFICERS OF THE 2ND MASSACHUSETTS

Corps with a Difference

Troops of XX Corps, chidingly called the "paper collar and white glove fellows" by others on the march, were the odd-men-out in Sherman's army. Mostly Easterners, they had not only fought in a different theater of the War, but also observed a far stricter code of discipline than the three other corps. The men of XX Corps were crisp in appearance and well practiced in drill, and at first they disparaged the more casual manner of the western troops. One XX Corps soldier wrote with disgust of the "raggedness and uncleanliness" of the men in the other corps. Another went even further: "The XX Corps has surpassed the Western Army as much in its fighting quality as it does in appearance, drill and discipline. It seems men can make a neat appearance on dress parade and fight well too."

But as the campaign wore on, the rigid discipline relaxed, and the differences between an Easterner and a Westerner grew less important. "When the time comes to stand up on the battle front," a corporal wrote, "there is no discount on either and one is anxious to have the other on hand."

CORPORAL JAMES HYDE, 137TH NEW YORK

ZOUAVES OF THE 33RD NEW JERSEY

PRIVATE ROBERT STRONG, 105TH ILLINOIS

Swath of Destruction

"Evidently it is a material element in this campaign to produce among the people of Georgia a thorough conviction of the personal misery which attends war, and of the utter helplessness and inability of their 'rulers,' State or Confederate, to protect them. And I am bound to say that I believe more and more that only by this means can the war be ended."

MAJOR HENRY HITCHCOCK OF GENERAL SHERMAN'S STAFF

2

"There are rumors," young Theodore Upson of the 100th Indiana wrote in his journal in Atlanta, "that we are to cut loose and march South to the Ocean." It was November 15, 1864, and Sherman's army was poised for its great adventure.

General Sherman had ridden into the city the previous afternoon to find all was in readiness. Since receiving Grant's permission to begin his long-planned march to the sea, Sherman had been at Kingston, Georgia, 50 miles to the northwest, busily speeding his army back toward Atlanta. He had ordered most of the immense stockpile of supplies there hauled back up to Chattanooga, leaving behind only what would fit in 2,500 light wagons. He had instructed the army's surgeons to examine every man with any history of illness — and officers every horse — to be sure they would be able to make it all the way to Savannah. "The sick were sent back to Chattanooga and Nashville, along with every pound of baggage that could be dispensed with," wrote Captain Daniel Oakey of the 2nd Massachusetts. "The army was reduced, one might say, to its fighting weight, no man being retained who was not capable of a long march." It was an army, another officer boasted, "composed of men whose bodies were so inured to hardship that disease could make no impression on them."

Before leaving Kingston, Sherman had also sent a last message to Grant, explaining once again the purpose of his extraordinary expedition. "If the North can march an army right through the South," he wired, "it is proof positive that the North can prevail." He signed off with humor: "I will not attempt to send couriers back, but trust to the Richmond papers to keep you well advised."

In addition, Sherman had a last-minute exchange of telegrams with General George Thomas in Nashville. Thomas was finally satisfied that he had enough men to hold off the Confederate army that was heading toward him across the Tennessee River. Indeed, Thomas had grown belligerent. He would "ruin" General Beauregard, he wired Sherman, "unless he gets out of the way very rapidly." And he wished Sherman Godspeed: "I am now convinced that your success will fully equal your expectations."

Sherman hurriedly replied "Dispatch received," and then instructed his telegraphers to cut the wires. No countermanding orders could reach him now. The last trains rolled northward, the engineers tooting their whistles and waving. Behind them bridges were burned and tracks ripped up.

The army was on its own, facing a perilous march of 225 miles, as the crow flies, through the heart of the Confederacy. The soldiers, wrote F. Y. Hedley, adjutant of the 32nd Illinois, knew they "were about to march out into a great unknown. It was a

Union troops gave this drum to 12-year-old Samuel Arms, a refugee slave from a Georgia plantation who was taken along as a drummer boy on Sherman's march to the sea. Though never officially recognized as a member of the U.S. Army, Arms continued to play the drum at military reviews after the War.

voyage upon untried waters, beyond which might lie no shore. They knew not what course they were to pursue, what dangers they were to meet, what enemies were to oppose them." And all were aware, Hedley continued, that "those who might fall would leave their bones in a strange and unfriendly land forever."

But the anxiety that the men felt at the prospect was counterbalanced by enthusiasm. "We are in fine shape and I think could go anywhere Uncle Billy would lead," wrote Theodore Upson. "There was something intensely exciting," recalled Captain Oakey, "in this perfect isolation."

But first they would destroy everything in Atlanta that might be of use to the Confederates when they reoccupied the city after Sherman's departure. Captain Orlando Poe, the army's chief engineer, had been busy demolishing railroad stations, warehouses and factories with a battering-ram of his own design — a 21-foot-long iron bar hanging by a chain from a 10-foot-high sawhorse. With this device, reported Major Henry Hitchcock, Sherman's assistant adjutant general, Poe had rammed down the stone and brick depot until it was a "perfect smash." On the evening of November 15, Poe and his men put Atlanta's industrial area to the torch.

The inferno spread, especially after the flames leaped through an oil refinery and then ignited some shells left in the wreckage of an arsenal; the shells exploded and hurled streamers of flame into the sky, setting other buildings on fire. From a headquarters window, Henry Hitchcock watched "immense and raging fires lighting up whole heavens — first bursts of smoke, dense, black volumes, then tongues of flame, then huge waves of fire roll up into the sky; presently

the skeletons of great warehouses stand out in relief against sheets of roaring, blazing, furious flames — then the angry waves roll less high, and are of a deeper color, then sink and cease."

Colonel Adin Underwood of the 33rd Massachusetts remembered the "crash of falling buildings, and the changes, as if by the turn of a kaleidoscope, of strong walls and proud structures into heaps of desolation." Underwood also recalled that his regiment's band played as the fires raged. The mixture of music with roaring flames and explosions "seemed like a demoniacal triumph over the fate of the city that had so long defied Sherman's armies." Reported David Conyngham of the New York *Herald:* "The heart was burning out of beautiful Atlanta."

Sherman had ordered that only Atlanta's business and industrial areas be destroyed. No dwellings would be torched and no fires started at all until he reached the city to supervise. Arsonists were to be shot on sight. But in fact civilian looters had been ransacking and then burning empty houses since November 11. Now more dwellings went up as sporadic looting continued and the flames spread from the industrial area into some residential neighborhoods. The *Herald's* Conyngham reported seeing soldiers batter down the doors of houses with rifle butts; steal tobacco, whiskey and other goods; then set fire to the structures. Such lawlessness might have been worse had not Sherman and some of his officers spent much of the night patrolling the streets, scaring off groups of would-be looters.

Sherman was caught in a paradox that would last the whole campaign. He and most of his men shrank from carrying out war on the Confederacy's civilian population. But Sherman's aim was destruction — to teach the South a painful object lesson in the futility of continuing the conflict. And the march across Georgia would bring out the worst in some men who, let loose on the countryside, reveled in the chance for plunder and set fire to farmhouses and mansions for the sheer pleasure of watching the buildings burn.

As the last fires died out in Atlanta, Sherman and the army's rear guard left the city, passing through 200 acres of ashy desolation. Sherman, his black, braidless hat jammed on his head, rode his favorite horse,

Sam. On a hill to the east he drew rein to look back. "Behind us lay Atlanta," he later wrote, "smouldering and in ruins, the black smoke rising high in the air and hanging like a pall." Captain Poe estimated that 37 percent of Atlanta was destroyed; the business and industrial sections were gone, but a majority of the residences were standing and most of the churches survived.

The people of the city would rebound quickly from the tragedy: Within three weeks a post office was open, newspapers were being published, rebuilding had begun and there was an adequate supply of food.

At the start of his march to the sea, General Sherman prepares to send a last message from Atlanta before ordering the telegraph wires cut, severing all communication with the North. Wrapped around the base of the pole are lengths of railroad track that were heated and twisted to render them useless, like the section shown above.

Atlanta was battered but far from dead.

As soon as Sherman turned his horse's head to the east, leaving Atlanta behind, his mood brightened remarkably. For the first time in his military career he was completely on his own; whatever happened in the weeks to come would be his doing and his alone, and this independence invigorated him. "The day was extremely beautiful," he remembered, "and an unusual feeling of exhilaration seemed to pervade all minds—a feeling of something to come, vague and undefined, still full of venture and intense interest. Even the common soldiers caught the inspiration, and many a group called out to me as I worked my way past them, 'Uncle Billy, I guess Grant is waiting for us at Richmond!' " As the men trudged along, bands played rousing marches. Row upon row of gun barrels glistened in the blazing Georgia sun and wagons topped with white canvas snaked away into the dusty distance.

Almost 62,000 soldiers were on the move, 55,000 of them on foot, 5,000 on cavalry horses and 2,000 riding caissons or the artillery horses that pulled the army's 65 guns. Each infantryman carried 40 rounds, and the wagon trains held another 200 rounds per man; ammunition could not be replaced, and Sherman was determined not to run out. The wagons also carried four pontoon bridges, for there were rivers to be crossed.

Rations, however, were meager for so ambitious a march: only 20 days' worth of salt pork, hardtack, coffee, salt and sugar. And there were only five days of oats and corn for the livestock—just enough to get the animals through the clean-picked area around Atlanta and into the fertile country beyond. Altogether it was a lean outfit. "Probably never were wagons of an army train more completely loaded with only the essentials required for a campaign," wrote a New York sergeant named Rice Bull.

It was also a youthful army, most of the men under voting age, and largely a Western outfit. Of the army's 218 regiments, 185 were from the farmlands of Ohio, Illinois, Indiana and other parts of the Midwest. Only 33 regiments had been raised in Eastern states. Perhaps because so many of the troops had been farmboys, their manners were informal. Disciplined in combat, they were free and easy on the march or in bivouac. Their leader could hardly insist on spit and polish. Sherman occasionally dressed in full uniform, but normally he wore an old blue coat and low-quarter shoes. "A general without boots!" one soldier marveled. The men loved him, for they knew he valued their lives: Sherman always preferred to outflank an enemy rather than make a bloody head-on attack.

As the troops stepped out on that sparkling November morning, they felt they were marching off on a lark that was sure to produce wonders and excitement. "Such an army as we have I doubt if ever was got together before," Upson wrote in his journal. "The boys are ready for a meal or a fight and don't seem to care which it is." A woman by the name of Lizzie Perkerson, who stood on her porch watching them pass, would remember: "They told us they were going to play smash with the Confederacy, just going to sweep it out at one lick."

The men's confidence emboldened Sherman but also heightened his sense of responsibility. His troops—and everyone back in the North—had expectations that Sherman would accomplish great things. "Success would be accepted as a matter of course,"

Sherman wrote, "whereas, should we fail, this 'march' would be adjudged the wild adventure of a crazy fool."

He would have to move constantly, because the army and its animals would exhaust the food and forage of the countryside as they went. He must make it to the sea and

Sherman had four corps. He divided them into wings of two corps each, which would march to the sea on separate but roughly parallel routes. The northern wing — XIV and XX Corps of the old Army of the Cumberland, commanded by Major General Henry W. Slocum — would head due east from

A Confederate arsenal in Atlanta, set aflame before Sherman's army left the city, erupts with an explosion on the night of November 15, 1864. Sherman wrote in his memoirs that the night was "made hideous by the bursting of shells," whose fragments came "uncomfortably close" to the house in which he was quartered.

On November 16, the last of Sherman's troops march east, past ruined buildings as Atlanta burns behind them. A band in the column struck up "John Brown's Body." Sherman said, "The men caught up the strain, and never before or since have I heard the chorus of 'Glory, glory, hallelujah!' done with more spirit, or in better harmony of time and place."

gain a coastal foothold so that he could be resupplied by the U.S. Navy. He had told Grant that the supply ships should look for him between Hilton Head and Savannah "around Christmastime" — which left him only six weeks to march 275 miles. He was embarked on what *The British Army & Navy Gazette* called "one of the most brilliant or one of the most foolish things ever performed by a military leader." If he failed, added the London *Herald*, he would be "the scoff of mankind."

Atlanta toward the town of Augusta. The southern wing, made up of XV and XVII Corps under the leadership of Major General Oliver O. Howard — the old Army of the Tennessee — would take a southeasterly course toward Macon. Sherman hoped that whatever forces the Confederates managed to muster in his front would rush to defend these important rail junctions. Then, after a week or so of marching, the two wings would change course and veer toward each other, converging on Milledgeville, Georgia's capital. Sherman's plan — a huge double feint — was designed to confuse the enemy and skirt Confederate strongholds.

The two-pronged advance would serve other purposes as well. It would afford each wing more room for foraging and avoid the crowding and delays that would inevitably result if the army moved as one column. And the deployment would enable the army to cut a broad swath of destruction sometimes 60 miles wide through central Georgia.

Sherman started out riding with the two corps of Henry Slocum's northern wing, soon to be styled the Army of Georgia. Slocum, a 37-year-old New Yorker and West Point graduate, was a prickly character; he had been posted to the Western Theater after heated disagreements with General Joseph Hooker, his superior officer in Virginia. Sherman liked Slocum, however, perhaps because his personality — which combined a lively sensibility with brusque military pro-

fessionalism — seemed much a reflection of Sherman's own.

One of Slocum's two subordinate commanders was Brigadier General Jefferson C. Davis, in charge of XIV Corps, an Indianan with a deadly temper that was not improved by the usual incredulous response to his name. Leading XX Corps was a luxuriantly bearded brigadier general named Alpheus S. Williams. A lawyer and judge before the War, Williams had proved himself a capable officer in a dozen important battles in Virginia and the west.

The southern wing of the army was less capably commanded. Its leader, Oliver O. Howard, had been put in charge of the Army of the Tennessee back in July when its brilliant and beloved leader, Major General James McPherson, was killed in the Battle of Atlanta. Although a trained professional — West Point, class of 1854 — and an efficient organizer, Howard had proved himself an

indifferent leader of men and a lackluster battlefield commander. It was his XI Corps that had been surprised and routed by Stonewall Jackson's flank attack at Chancellorsville in 1863. And Howard's devout Christian beliefs — his men dubbed him "Old Prayer Book" — could not have recommended him to Sherman, who was distinctly a skeptic in religious matters.

But Sherman doubtless admired Howard's personal courage: He had lost his right arm leading a charge at Fair Oaks in 1862. Besides, if all went according to plan, neither wing of the army would have to fight a major battle on the way to Savannah; the objective was to keep the troops moving, and Howard could do that.

Howard's corps commanders were both men of considerable experience. Major General Peter J. Osterhaus, leading XV Corps, was a German immigrant with a Prussian military education. At the head of XVII Corps was Major General Francis Preston Blair Jr., a bluff, energetic Missourian, a former Congressman and chief of the House Military Affairs Committee. Blair had just returned to the Army after working in Lincoln's campaign for reelection.

Riding well ahead of Howard's wing, and screening the advance, was the 5,000-man cavalry division commanded by a daring but sometimes foolhardy young brigadier general named Hugh Judson Kilpatrick. A small, arrogant man with a lantern jaw and oversize sideburns the color of sand, Kilpatrick had earned the sobriquet "Kill Cavalry" for his habit of wearing out his troopers and their mounts on long rides and getting them slaughtered in furious charges. He had been an ardent amateur actor when he was at West Point and was theatrical in everything he did, including the fervent pursuit of women.

In a fight, however, Kilpatrick could be a formidable adversary. If attacked suddenly, wrote Major General Jacob D. Cox, who had observed Kilpatrick during the Atlanta Campaign, "he was quite capable of mounting bareback the first animal, horse or mule, that came to hand and charging in his shirt at the head of his troopers with a dare-devil recklessness that dismayed his opponents and imparted his own daring to his men." General Sherman summed it up: "I know that Kilpatrick is a hell of a damned fool, but I want just that sort of man to command my cavalry on this expedition."

Kilpatrick's men were ready, their horses rested and well fed, as they rode southeast down Georgia's roads, leading Howard's infantry columns toward Macon. Soon the Federal troopers were meeting their counterparts, lean veteran horsemen in faded gray. The Confederate cavalrymen threw up a succession of roadblocks — at East Point, Rough and Ready, Jonesboro, Stockbridge and Lovejoy's Station — in attempts to slow the Federal advance. But there were simply too many Federal horsemen and they came on with too much force. A Georgia cavalryman, Lieutenant John S. Ash, remembered, "We were so completely run over that we were scattered in every direction, those of us who were not killed or captured."

The leader of the Confederate cavalry lacked Kilpatrick's dramatic flair but was otherwise the Union general's match in every way. Major General Joseph Wheeler, a 28-year-old West Pointer, had gained the respect of officers on both sides for his superb leadership of the Army of Tennessee's cavalry. He weighed about 120 pounds — "a very small, very erect man," recalled Ella Mitch-

"Uncle Billy" and His Generals

The nickname of "Uncle Billy," conferred on General Sherman by his troops, signified both familiarity and respect. "Although he was pronounced crazy at one time," a soldier wrote, "I wish all Generals were afflicted as he is." Sherman's principal subordinates, however, failed to command the same degree of admiration. Henry Slocum, who led the left wing, though well regarded as a corps commander, was thought by some to be unsuited to head a larger force. "Slocum is about played out," a young lieutenant wrote. "Prosperity has been too much for him."

The pious attitudes of Oliver Howard, the right wing commander, caused grumblings among his men, who took to calling him "Old Prayer Book."

Sherman's corps commanders also earned harsh criticism from their men. Jefferson C. Davis' haphazard discipline moved one corporal to write: "I do think our Government is hard up when such men are allowed to command." Alpheus Williams, known as "Pops" to the men of his XX Corps, was once described as looking like "a dull old doctor, who loves good whiskey, with a disposition to the gout." In XV Corps, the Prussian ways of Peter Osterhaus, a German immigrant, did not sit well with his rough-edged western troops, who took to shouting "sow-belly!" behind the general's back. Similarly, the men of XVII Corps felt that their commander, General Francis Blair, herded them on unnecessary marches. On the road, the men would fill the air with sheeplike bleatings of "Blaa-aa-ir! Blaa-aa-ir!"

MAJOR GENERAL WILLIAM SHERMAN

MAJOR GENERAL HENRY W. SLOCUM

MAJOR GENERAL OLIVER O. HOWARD

BRIGADIER GENERAL
JEFFERSON C. DAVIS

BRIGADIER GENERAL
ALPHEUS S. WILLIAMS

BRIGADIER GENERAL
JUDSON KILPATRICK

MAJOR GENERAL
PETER J. OSTERHAUS

MAJOR GENERAL
FRANCIS P. BLAIR JR.

ell, a child who observed him, "dressed in grey, wearing a crimson sash and a large black plumed hat." He rarely smiled and seemed always to be in a hurry; he was, said one of his officers, "as restless as a disembodied spirit and as active as a cat." Wheeler liked to fight and so did his rough, undisciplined men, who sometimes provoked as much terror among Southern civilians as did the enemy. Wheeler commanded a force of 3,500 troopers. Most of the time the men were scattered widely, hovering around the Union columns, ahead and behind, impotent to stop the Federal advance but quick to snatch up stragglers, whom they often killed with little compunction.

As Kilpatrick's cavalry approached Macon, Wheeler concentrated about 2,000 of his horsemen for the defense of the city. Four miles from Macon's outskirts, the dismounted Confederate troopers dug in behind a set of earthworks to await a Federal attack. Kilpatrick did not disappoint them, his men attacking Wheeler's line with convincing fury. Kilpatrick then pulled back, well satisfied that he had fooled the enemy into thinking that the rest of Sherman's army was poised to attack the place.

For his part, Wheeler was sure that his spirited defense had helped save Macon, where even then a number of Confederate leaders were gathering, intent on concerting some plan that would stop or at least slow the Federal advance. Governor Joseph Brown had come from Milledgeville; former Governor Howell Cobb had also arrived, along with Robert Toombs, a onetime Confederate secretary of state. Ready to help Wheeler defend Macon was Major General Gustavus W. Smith with his Georgia militia, about 3,000 sketchily trained volunteers, many of them boys and overage farmers. General William Hardee had come from Savannah to take command of these inadequate defensive forces, and Lieutenant General Richard Taylor, a veteran of Lee's army in Virginia, had arrived to examine the gloomy situation and report to Richmond.

Howell Cobb met Taylor at the Macon railroad station and reported that Sherman's main body had been a dozen miles away the day before. Taylor suspected not. Had Sherman intended to attack Macon, he told Cobb, "you'd have seen him last night. He'd have come before you had time to finish the works or move your stores."

Sherman, sure enough, did not attack Macon. His failure to appear there threw the Confederates into a quandary. Their only hope of delaying the Federal march was now to concentrate what slender forces they possessed: Wheeler's cavalrymen, Gustavus Smith's militia and a few other isolated detachments. But where should they prepare to make a stand?

None of the officers nominally in charge took any decisive action. General Braxton Bragg, Chief of Staff, in Richmond, issued no orders and neither did General Beauregard, whose attention was divided between Georgia and John Bell Hood's Confederate advance into Tennessee to the west. General Hardee, ranking officer on the scene, recognized, as had Richard Taylor, that Sherman had merely feinted toward Macon and that his real objective was either Augusta or Savannah. Hardee left Macon for the coast, ordering General Smith to avoid battle and to march his pitiful little band of militiamen straight for Augusta to help in its defense — instructions that in a short time would be disobeyed at great cost.

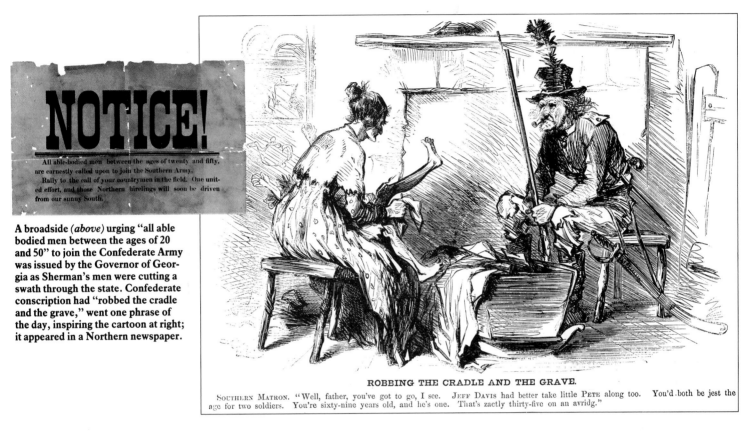

A broadside (*above*) urging "all able bodied men between the ages of 20 and 50" to join the Confederate Army was issued by the Governor of Georgia as Sherman's men were cutting a swath through the state. Confederate conscription had "robbed the cradle and the grave," went one phrase of the day, inspiring the cartoon at right; it appeared in a Northern newspaper.

ROBBING THE CRADLE AND THE GRAVE.

SOUTHERN MATRON. "Well, father, you've got to go, I see. JEFF DAVIS had better take little PETE along too. You'd both be jest the age for two soldiers. You're sixty-nine years old, and he's one. That's zactly thirty-five on an avridg."

After threatening Macon, Howard's wing circled to the northeast; the Federal army's other wing, under Slocum, approached Covington on its feint down the Georgia Railroad toward Augusta. Both wings were moving steadily and efficiently. "Skirmishers were in advance, flankers were out, and foraging parties were ahead gathering supplies from the rich plantations," wrote Captain Oakey. "We were expected to make 15 miles a day; to corduroy the roads where necessary; to destroy such property as was designated by our corps commander, and to consume everything eatable by man or beast."

Foraging parties — about 20 to 30 men under an officer — were sent out every morning by each regiment. The officers were mounted and usually so were their men, most of them riding horses or mules that had been picked up along the way. The mounts gave the foragers greater mobility to sweep the countryside for provisions — and to escape should they encounter strong detachments of Wheeler's cavalry. The officers knew the route the main column would take during the day and where to rejoin it at sundown. They also had a good idea of where other foraging parties were headed. If one got into trouble, the others nearby would close in on the sound of firing.

Sherman's standing orders were to "forage liberally on the country," seizing "whatever is needed by the command." He expressly forbade trespassing in "the dwellings of inhabitants," however, and also instructed the foragers to discriminate "between the rich who are usually hostile, and the poor and industrious, usually neutral or friendly." In either case, the troops were to leave behind "a reasonable portion" of a family's food "for their maintenance."

The men enthusiastically followed Sherman's order to forage liberally. But they tended to flout those instructions that urged restraint. A party, swooping down upon a farm or plantation, would clean out the smokehouse, kill all the chickens and hogs, empty the corncribs and oatbins, seize the flour supply and commandeer any delicacies they found, such as crocks of butter or honey. These edibles would be loaded on whatever carts or wagons came to hand. The troops would then round up any livestock they wanted. The more vengeful foraging parties would slaughter the rest. In any case, many a farm or plantation family found it had precious little left to eat.

Dolly Sumner Lunt Burge, a widow and mistress of a large plantation, recorded what it meant to be a rich landowner in the path of the army. As Federal troops approached her house, located on the Madison road nine miles east of Covington, she stood by her gate. "But like Demons they rushed in! My yards are full. To my smoke-house, my Dairy, Pantry, Kitchen and Cellar, like famished wolves they come, breaking locks and whatever is in their way. The thousand pounds of meat in my smoke-house is gone in a twinkling, my flour, my meat, my lard, butter, eggs, pickles both in vinegar and brine, wine, jars, and jugs, are all gone. My eighteen fat turkeys, my hens, chickens and fowl, my young pigs, are shot down in my yard and hunted as if they were the rebels themselves."

Trespass in the Southern homes was also common. All too frequently the troops ransacked houses, smashing and pilfering drawers and cabinets. The foragers also searched yards and garden plots for boxes containing jewels, silver or choice foodstuffs that the owners had buried. Any freshly turned earth was quickly investigated. The troops used ramrods or bayonets to probe for valuables. It was comical, one officer later wrote, to see battle-hardened veterans "punching the unoffending earth in an apparently idiotic but certainly most energetic way."

Sometimes slaves volunteered to reveal their owners' hiding places, and envious neighbors were known to do the same. Occasionally the troops, sure of finding treasure, discovered something else. A party of men from the 2nd Minnesota shouted with joy when a ramrod, probing a freshly dug spot, thumped on something solid. The Minnesotans eagerly uncovered a wooden box and opened it — only to fall back from the stench of a dead dog. "It looks like poor Curly will get no peace," a woman said. "That's the fourth time he's been dug up today."

For their amusement, the foragers frequently snatched clothes and family heirlooms that were of little practical value. Soldiers were seen returning from foraging expeditions dressed in regimentals from the Revolutionary War, complete with tricorn hat and wig. Others came back decked out in low-necked evening gowns, or in beaver hats and old-fashioned swallow-tailed coats. For many of the men the entire march was prime sport. "This is probably the most gigantic pleasure expedition ever planned," wrote one of Howard's veterans. And a soldier remarked, "I wouldn't have missed it for fifty dollars."

Still, there were dangers in foraging.

Alexander Shannon's Ferocious Scouts

"In the morning we found 3 Yanks driving off a lady's cows. We soon scattered their brains and moved on." So wrote Private Enoch D. John, a member of a company of the 8th Texas Cavalry that, under Captain Alexander Shannon, came to be known as Shannon's Scouts. Organized for reconnaissance, the hand-picked 30-man outfit soon undertook audacious raids on Sherman's foraging parties, sometimes attacking units four times its size. Shannon's Scouts shadowed the Union army across Georgia, killing 43 Federals and capturing 102. Captain Shannon became such a thorn in the Union's side that General Judson Kilpatrick offered a $5,000 reward for his capture. Later, under a flag of truce, Shannon acknowledged Kilpatrick's offer saying, "I want to thank you for the signal honor, but I'm going to go you one better: I'm going to get you for nothing." Some months later, at Monroe's Crossroads, Shannon nearly made good on his promise when a midnight raid sent Kilpatrick fleeing without his horse and clothes.

Captain Alexander Shannon (*top*) commanded the cavalry unit known as Shannon's Scouts, some of whose troopers are shown here.

The joyous slaves of a Georgia plantation greet their liberators with gifts of food and flowers. One of Sherman's officers (*left*) doffs his hat to disdainful ladies of the plantation in this painting by Thomas Nast.

Small details surprised at their work by detachments of Wheeler's cavalry had to fight furiously to escape. If captured, the Federals were often summarily executed. During the march, the bodies of at least 64 Union soldiers were found hanged, shot in the head at close range or with their throats slit, often with signs pinned to their uniforms reading "Death to all Foragers."

The women of Georgia were generally frightened by the foragers, but many remained proudly defiant. "Our men will fight you as long as they live," a woman standing with her children told Federal soldiers, "and these boys'll fight you when they grow up." An Iowa soldier remembered a young woman who cried, "You can kill us, but you can't conquer us." The soldiers believed Southern women were the real impetus behind the War. An Ohio colonel heard one of his men lecture a farmwoman: "You urge young men to the battlefield where men are being killed by the thousands, while you stay home and sing *The Bonnie Blue Flag;* but you set up a howl when you see the Yankees down here getting your chickens. Many of your young men have told us that they are tired of war and would quit, but you women would shame them and drive them back."

The wealthier Georgia landowners lost more than their livestock and provisions. They lost in many cases their human property, their slaves. It was at Covington that the army first experienced an outpouring of blacks — an occurrence that would become familiar as the march continued. Black men and women, old, young, children, elders with gray hair, all came out to greet the men they saw as their liberators. They came laughing, crying, cheering, shouting and

praying. They had been told that Federal soldiers made it a practice to burn black men and drown their women and children, but now they showed no fear. A Michigan drummer boy remembered a woman throwing her arms around him and crying, "They told us this here army was devils from hell but praise the Lord, it's the Lord's own babes and sucklings." Another soldier heard a slave cry out with ringing fervency at the sight of the U.S. flag, "My God, did you ever see such a pretty thing!"

Sherman was welcomed as the deliverer promised in the Bible. "I have seen the great Messiah and the Army of the Lord!" one white-haired man shouted. Sherman re-

called that "the Negroes were simply frantic with joy. Whenever they heard my name, they clustered about my horse, shouted and prayed in their peculiar style which had a natural eloquence that would have moved a stone." Sherman asked one elderly slave if he understood about the War. The man nodded. He had been looking for the "angel of the Lord" since he was a child. He knew, he continued, that the Federals professed to be fighting for the Union, but he supposed slavery was the real cause of the War — and that if the Union was victorious, he would be free. "I asked him," Sherman recalled, "if all the negro slaves comprehended this fact, and he said: they surely did."

As Sherman's army approaches, frightened Southerners make a mad dash, clutching a few possessions and driving a couple of sheep ahead of them. "It is a terrible thing," wrote Major Henry Hitchcock, an aide of Sherman's, "to see the terror and grief of these women and children."

The slaves turned out by the thousands to meet the Federals. They waited at every crossing, they lined the roads and they poured through the camps at night, bringing provisions, information and adoration.

Slocum's northern wing, followed by an ever-growing column of liberated blacks, marched on to the lovely little town of Madison, where roses and dahlias were in bloom. On November 17, as slaves cheered, the troops set fire to the depot and a slave-pen, including the whips and paddles found there, and resumed their march to the east, roses woven into garlands for their hats and thrust into the barrels of their rifles.

Soon the lead brigades came to a large plantation owned by a man named Farrar. He was away — most of the able-bodied men had hurried off, much to the amused contempt of the slaves — but Mrs. Farrar was there. The Farrar slaves told Major Henry Hitchcock they had been habitually punished by flogging not only with straps but also "with hand-saws and paddles with holes — and salt put in the wounds. They also told us of a famous 'track-hound' (bloodhound) at the next house, nearby, used to hunt runaways." The hound, a large red dog, was shot by Sherman's order, to the great glee of the Farrar slaves.

The Federal soldiers formed a special hatred for such tracking dogs, knowing that slaveowners used the animals to hunt not only runaway slaves but also escaping Federal prisoners of war. The troops killed these dogs whenever they came across them and frequently killed house pets as well. They also managed to acquire a stunning number of animals — dogs, cats, gamecocks, goats, donkeys, raccoons, possums and even pigs — as pets of their own, so that soon every company had a mascot.

As the first week of the march came to an end, the two wings of the army turned toward each other, as planned, to converge on the state capital, Milledgeville. On the way there, Sherman found himself on a lush 6,000-acre plantation that he learned was the property of Howell Cobb, the former Governor, who was in Macon trying to figure out how to defend his state. Federal foragers had already removed the easily portable supplies, Hitchcock noted, but there was "plenty

A Northern cartoon mocks a Southerner's expectation of loyalty from a slave. Not all slaveowners had such delusions; some referred to their slaves disdainfully as "Sherman's reinforcements."

DOWN IN GEORGIA—SHERMAN'S MARCH.

DARKEY—" Oh, massa, dere's Sherman's army coming up to de front stoop."
MASTER—" Well, Cæsar, take this gun and keep 'em off till I'm well away."

left—fodder, corn, oats, bins full of peanuts—twenty sacks fine salt—500 gallons or more of sorghum molasses."

Sherman, who placed the blame for the start of the War on Cobb and other Southern politicians of his ilk, decided to strip the place thoroughly. He told the slaves and soldiers on the scene to take what they wanted and to burn the rest. "Of course we confiscated his property," Sherman remembered. "I sent back word to General Davis to explain whose plantation it was and instructed him to spare nothing. That night huge bonfires consumed the fence rails to keep our soldiers warm."

Meanwhile to the south, just 10 miles east of Macon, one of the few battles to occur during the trek from Atlanta to Savannah was shaping up. On the morning of November 22, the ragtag brigades of Georgia militia, on their way to the coast as ordered, were approaching the town of Griswoldville. General Smith had remained in Macon arranging for supplies, and in temporary command of the Confederate troops was a novice brigadier named P. J. Phillips.

Directly in the Georgians' path was a single brigade of Federal infantry acting as rear guard for General Osterhaus' XV Corps. The brigade numbered only 1,513 men— half the size of the Confederate force— but they were veteran campaigners, and one regiment was armed with Spencer repeating rifles. Their leader, Brigadier General Charles C. Walcutt, an efficient and prudent officer from Ohio, had ordered his troops to construct temporary timberworks on a hill just beyond Griswoldville in case roving Confederate troopers attacked.

Phillips and his green militiamen had been instructed to avoid an engagement with the enemy. But Phillips was either nervous or hungry for glory—or possibly, as some of his men later said, having a bout with the bottle. He determined that his militiamen, untrained and ill-armed as they were, outnumbered the troops in Walcutt's brigade, and he decided to attack. As the Federals cooked their noon meal in a grove of trees, Phillips led his men into an open field and deployed them for the assault.

The Federals among the trees looked up in astonishment to see a line of Confederates coming toward them. A second line followed, and a third, crossing a stubbled field in front of Walcutt's well-placed works. The Georgians held their fire and it was so quiet as they approached that the Federals could hear the enemy officers giving their commands. Walcutt coolly waited until the first line was very close before he allowed his men to shoot. A Federal volley ripped through the first line, but the survivors returned the

Union soldiers, acting on the order of their commander, kill a pair of bloodhounds found on a Georgia plantation. The unpleasant scene was repeated throughout Sherman's march in the belief that most hounds had been used to track runaway slaves and escaped Federal prisoners.

fire and marched forward without wavering, the rear lines following steadily. The repeating rifles opened a savage fire and the Confederates fell in droves. But those not hit continued to move forward, too inexperienced to realize what was happening.

Young Theodore Upson was in Walcutt's brigade. "I never saw our boys fight better than they did then," Upson recalled. "Once when we were so hard pressed that it seemed as though they were going to run over us by sheer force of numbers our boys put on their bayonets and resolved to hold their ground at any cost." The rapid fire emptied the Federals' cartridge boxes, and drummer boys ran for more ammunition. The incredible charge came within 50 yards — murderous range — before it broke. There was a ravine nearby and the remaining Georgians bolted for it, then retreated eastward.

Later an Illinois captain, Charles Wills, walked onto the field. "Old grey haired and weakly looking men and little boys, not over 15 years old, lay dead or writhing in pain," he wrote. "I hope," Wills added, "we will never have to shoot at such men again. They knew nothing at all about fighting, and I think their officers knew as little."

Gustavus Smith, bitterly angry at this useless wasting of lives, reported Phillips' losses as 51 killed, 472 wounded. Federal casualties totaled 13 men dead and 79 wounded. Among the Federal dead was the elderly "Uncle" Aaron Wolford, the patriarch of Upson's company. The night before, Upson remembered, Wolford had expressed a premonition of death and requested that Upson tend to his possessions. Upson was beside Wolford when a bullet struck the older man's head. He had been like a father to the young men in the company, and Upson

could not bear to see him buried in a common grave. He found a hollow sycamore log and split it to make a coffin.

In Milledgeville, alarm reigned as the Federal army neared. "Thick and fast the rumors flew," reported a woman who signed herself Miss A. C. Cooper. "The excitement increased; we could neither eat nor sleep. Scouts were sent out up this road, down that, across the country." In the town itself, she continued, "women cried and prayed, babies yelled, dogs howled, mules brayed, Negro drivers swore — we rushed out on the front veranda and listened for the guns. We could not have heard a cannon, for from every house came the sound of weeping and heart-rending cries."

The state legislature decided that the wise course was to get out of town before Sherman arrived. Governor Brown, back from Macon, busied himself loading furniture from the governor's mansion on the last train to leave town. The legislature met in panic preparatory to its own flight. "Such a body of representatives made my cheeks glow with shame," wrote Anna Maria Green, daughter of the superintendent of the state asylum. "They could not stand for the defense of their own capital."

There were approximately 650 Confederate troops in Milledgeville — mostly schoolboys and convicts released from the penitentiary — under the command of Brigadier General Harry Wayne. Wayne wisely recognized the impossibility of repulsing the Federal army and ordered his ragtag soldiers to march eastward. Perhaps they could be of help in the defense of Savannah.

Most of Milledgeville's civilian inhabitants decided to remain despite their fear of General Sherman, whom Miss Cooper described as "a huge octopus who stretched out his long arms and gathered everything in, leaving only ruin and desolation." As the last of Wayne's Confederates left, three scouts, "their horses white with foam, flashed by shouting a 'goodbye'," Miss Cooper wrote. The first of the Federal troops were not far behind. "Bullets thick as hail whistled past us, burying themselves in the pillars and back of the veranda where we stood so paralyzed we could not move."

On the afternoon of November 22, the 107th New York raised its flag over the capitol. Sherman and his staff, arriving the next day, spent a night in the now-bare governor's mansion, using planks placed across the backs of camp chairs for tables, and sleeping on the floor. He found in the mansion the first newspapers he had seen since he had left Atlanta; editors throughout the Confederacy were proving fiery verbal fighters, assuring the people that Sherman and his Federal army were doomed. Sherman reported that he was amused, but many of his men were angered by this bombast.

Young officers from New York and Wisconsin staged a mock session in the legislative chamber. Some were having "bourbon fits," according to an onlooker, as they repealed the state's Ordinance of Secession and then at the shout "The Yankees are coming!" fled in panic, in a parody of the recently departed legislators. Soldiers roamed the statehouse, scattering papers and hurling state library books from the windows — "a very bad exhibition of a very lawless nature," as Sergeant Stephen Fleharty of the 102nd Illinois reported. "An army is a terrible engine and hard to control," concurred Henry Hitchcock.

Despite a considerable chorus of com-plaint from the city's residents at such behavior — the "vandals left suffering and desolation behind them," wrote diarist Anna Maria Green — the damage done to Milledgeville was minor. Rumors that the Federals were planning to burn the place turned out to be false, although the arsenal and ammunition magazine were destroyed in explosions that damaged some nearby structures. The Federal occupation was also brief. Sherman rode southeastward from the city on November 24, the left wing following him on roads that headed in the direction of Savannah. General Howard's right wing, which had approached within 14 miles of Milledgeville at the town of Gordon, had already turned toward Savannah, still marching on a path roughly parallel to the other column.

As the army slogged on, Sherman reduced the required day's march from 15 miles to 10 so that foragers would have extra time to gather supplies — and other troops could more thoroughly destroy railroad tracks, mills, cotton gins and anything else useful to the Confederacy's war effort. The most difficult of the tasks was railroad wrecking. Working in shifts, the men of one division and then another would pry up the rails with crowbars. The ties, recalled Sergeant Rice Bull, "would be gathered and piled up crosswise to a height of four feet with the rails placed on top. When the ties were fired the rails would become red hot and could be twisted and destroyed." A division, working hard, could wreck 10 miles of road in a day. The pine-wood ties, Sergeant Bull remembered, burned like pitch and the smoke covered "our hands and faces with a black veneer that could only be removed by soap and water, and we had no soap."

Except for Wheeler's harassing horsemen,

A color sergeant of the 107th New York stands with his regiment's tattered flag on the roof of the state capitol at Milledgeville, Georgia, on November 22, 1864. "The Legislature was in session the day before," an Ohio soldier wrote dryly, "but they adjourned in great rapidity to meet again when convenient."

there was little danger from the enemy. The only organized opposition that loomed was Harry Wayne's force of 650 boys and convicts. Wayne briefly planned to make a stand at the Oconee River, but as Sherman's right wing bore down on his paltry force, the hopelessness of his position became painfully apparent. After firing a few volleys at the approaching Federals, the Confederates abandoned their Oconee line.

Slocum's two corps then crossed on pontoon bridges, as a 55th Illinois soldier put it,

"noisily gay, keeping up an incessant roar, singing, shouting and imitating the cries of bird and beast." The men entered new country, a marshy land drained by the Oconee and Ogeechee Rivers and studded with pine barrens where the forests grew thick and gloomy. The troops saw Spanish moss for the first time. Gone were the rich fields and large plantations that had filled foragers' wagons with booty: This country had a poor look, in land and people alike.

In one tumble-down cabin, an 18-year-old

While soldiers pry up track and set fire to rail cars and depot buildings, an officer on horseback scans further scenes of destruction through his telescope; there, in the

...istance, soldiers are driving off cattle and destroying a bridge. In the foreground, at right, a refugee slave family seeks aid.

captain named Charles Belknap and his foraging party found two abandoned girls, three and five years of age, able only to wail, "Mama gone, mama gone." Belknap and his men built a fire, heated water to give the grimy children a bath, washed their hair and fed them. The young captain then took the waifs to nearby cabins, but none of the neighbors would take the little girls in. Finally the soldiers stole clothing for the children, who had been dressed only in sacks, put them on the back of a pack mule and carried them along to Savannah as mascots.

Eventually the children were taken North by a wounded officer on furlough, and homes were found for them there.

In 10 days the army had covered nearly half the distance to Savannah with almost no opposition. Sherman moved his headquarters to General Howard's right wing, traveling with Frank Blair's XVII Corps while Howard rode with Osterhaus' XV Corps. Since the threat from Confederates at Macon was past, Kilpatrick's cavalry moved over to the left wing to demonstrate toward Augusta, threaten the garrison there and prevent

General Judson Kilpatrick, with saber upraised, leads a cavalry charge at Waynesboro, Georgia, against the forces of Joseph Wheeler on December 4, 1864. "A cavalry fight," one Federal officer declared, "is just about as much fun as a fox hunt."

Confederate Brigadier General Pierce Manning Butler Young, in command of Wade Hampton's old division, boldly, but vainly, tried to defend both Augusta and Savannah. For these actions he received a promotion, making him the youngest major general in the Confederate Army.

those troops from moving out to harass the Federal rear. The only substantial force ahead was the 10,000 men under Hardee at Savannah—and the roving troopers under Joseph Wheeler, still a threat.

On the night of November 26, near Augusta, Kilpatrick discovered just how dangerous Wheeler could be. Wheeler's horsemen suddenly overrode a Federal cavalry campsite at Sylvan Grove, galloping among the sleeping troopers and taking prisoners, regimental colors and about 50 horses. Kilpatrick himself was staying at a nearby house; he managed to escape—with shirttails flying, his horse leaping over fences.

Fighting continued for the next three days in a series of skirmishes that came to be known collectively as the Battle of Waynesboro. Kilpatrick had come too close to Augusta, and Wheeler's men buzzed around the various units of Federal cavalry like swarms

of angry hornets. On November 27 Kilpatrick and his troopers had to fight for their lives, barely holding off repeated attacks by Wheeler. Squadrons of troopers galloped head on into each other, sabers clashing and pistols cracking at close range. By Wheeler's account, his men killed, wounded or captured 200 Federal cavalrymen. Then on November 28 Kilpatrick himself again barely escaped capture when he and a single regiment, the 9th Michigan Cavalry, were surprised by most of Wheeler's corps and had to fight their way to the main body of Union troopers. Finally prudence overcame vainglory and Kilpatrick humbly asked the infantry for help.

To the rescue came two brigades of Federal foot soldiers. "Kilpatrick drew up his whole division of cavalry in the open fields this morning at 7 o'clock," wrote Major James Connolly, a divisional staff officer who was there. Kilpatrick's men "whipped Wheeler soundly," Connolly continued, "killing, wounding and capturing about 300 of his men, and losing only about 50 themselves." But then, Connolly added with the amused disdain that infantrymen reserved for the cavalry, "Kilpatrick's men had the moral support of two of our brigades that were formed in line right behind them and kept moving forward as they moved, so that our cavalry all the time knew that there was no chance of their being whipped." After driving Wheeler's main body up the railroad track to Waynesboro and then through the town, Kilpatrick's troopers checked other Confederate riders at a place called Reynolds' Plantation. With that Kilpatrick and his men joined Slocum's columns on the roads leading to Savannah.

The next sizable town on the route for Slocum was Millen, a railroad junction on the far side of the Ogeechee River and the site of a large prisoner-of-war compound that was called Camp Lawton. Slocum hoped, of course, to rescue the thousands of Federal prisoners being held there. But Kilpatrick's advance brigade, scouting ahead of the infantry, arrived at the river just in time to see emaciated prisoners being herded into boxcars on the opposite shore.

During the two days that XIV and XX Corps rested in Millen, the troops had ample time to inspect Camp Lawton and found it a cruel, repellent place. The only shelters were a few makeshift huts — "miserable hovels hardly fit for swine," said an army chaplain. Most of the prisoners had lived in holes dug in the ground. "Some were quite large where several men were together," recalled Sergeant Rice Bull; others were just large enough for a single man "to crawl in and have protection from storm and cold." A punishment shed had stocks that looked as if they had been used often. A sign by a freshly filled-in trench said "650 Buried Here." One officer wrote: "Everyone who visited this place came away with a feeling of hardness toward the Southern Confederacy he had never felt before." The Federals burned the stockade and, venting their anger, a good part of Millen as well.

The troops had seen other dismaying evidence that their captured compatriots were being ill-treated in Southern stockades. Several days earlier, in Milledgeville, the troops had been eating a Thanksgiving feast of turkey and chicken when several escaped Federal prisoners tottered into town. They had somehow fled the notorious prison camp at Andersonville, Georgia, and crossed 100 miles of enemy territory without detection.

They were scarecrows in rags, recalled Colonel Charles D. Kerr of the 16th Illinois Cavalry; they had "a wild animal stare" in their eyes and wept at the smell of food and the sight of the U.S. flag. His troops were "sickened and infuriated," wrote Colonel Kerr, by the sight of the pitiful escapees.

Such incidents doubtless contributed to the increasing violence and cruelty that marked the second half of the army's march across Georgia. So did reports of barbarities committed by Wheeler's cavalrymen. The Federal troops were also angered by the Georgia newspaper editorials and articles urging noncombatants to murder any Federals they could waylay. "Let every man fly to arms," read one printed exhortation, and "assail the invader." The Savannah *Daily Morning News* recommended that straggling Yankees "be beautifully bushwhacked."

In any event, the regular foraging parties seemed to grow rougher and meaner. Mary Jones Mallard, a clergyman's daughter, described the invasion of her mother's Liberty County plantation by a berserk crew of foragers. "About four in the afternoon we heard the clash of arms and noise of horsemen and by the time Mother and I could get down stairs we saw forty or fifty men in the pantry, flying hither and thither, ripping open the safe with their swords and breaking open the crockery cupboards." The foragers then "flew around the house tearing open boxes, everything that was closed. They broke open Mother's little work table with an andiron hoping to find money or jewelry.

"It was vain to utter a word," Mrs. Mallard continued, "for we were completely paralyzed by the fury of these ruffians. It is impossible to imagine the horrible uproar, all yelling, cursing, quarreling and running

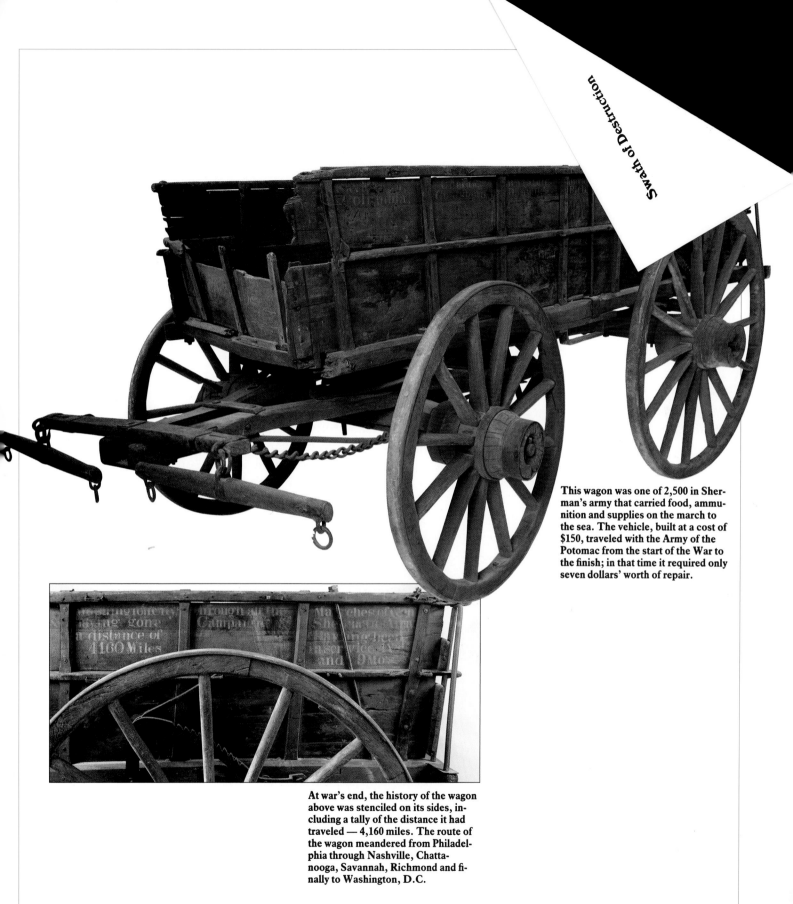

This wagon was one of 2,500 in Sherman's army that carried food, ammunition and supplies on the march to the sea. The vehicle, built at a cost of $150, traveled with the Army of the Potomac from the start of the War to the finish; in that time it required only seven dollars' worth of repair.

At war's end, the history of the wagon above was stenciled on its sides, including a tally of the distance it had traveled — 4,160 miles. The route of the wagon meandered from Philadelphia through Nashville, Chattanooga, Savannah, Richmond and finally to Washington, D.C.

from one room to another in wild confusion. Such was their blasphemous language, their horrible countenances, that we realized what must be the association of the lost in the world of eternal woe."

Worse than the regular foragers were unsanctioned gangs of renegades and looters that appeared as the army moved eastward. Some of the gang members were Federal troops who had separated from their commands and seldom reported to any officer — an underclass of hobo soldiers. They were often joined by vagrant Georgia civilians, by Confederate deserters and in some cases by troopers from Wheeler's cavalry units. Most Federal troops stayed with their units and many deplored the activities of these "bummers," as the renegades came to be called.

Indeed, there were sharp confrontations as decent soldiers tried to protect women and children from the roving looters. But the gangs of bummers grew, following and moving parallel with the army.

The bummers rode stolen horses and their aim, aside from sheer destruction, was whiskey and gold. In one case, a group of them hanged an elderly farmer until he was nearly dead only to lay hands on his gold watch. They smashed pianos and valuable furniture with rifle butts and probably set fire to more houses in Georgia than did all of the regular foraging parties combined. And they were probably responsible for a majority of the rapes committed during the march.

Officers made sporadic attempts to punish the worst offenders. General Jefferson C.

Running wild on a Georgia farm, men of a Union foraging party slaughter livestock and cart off hay. One plantation owner, who hid in the woods and watched while Federals swarmed over his property, likened the scene to "the destruction of Jerusalem on a small scale."

A "bummer," the nickname given to certain unscrupulous foragers during Sherman's march, returns to camp on muleback, loaded down with goods in this sketch by Henry Otis Dwight, a soldier of the 20th Ohio.

Davis of XIV Corps threatened to execute looters, which outraged his men, who already suspected him of being a Southern sympathizer. In any case, Davis executed no one. General Howard threatened to shoot looters, as well, but backed down, commuting the sentence when a court martial condemned one of his soldiers to death. General Osterhaus fined men a month's pay for looting and General Blair took similar action.

Sherman insisted later that he had wanted foraging, not pillaging. As he explained it, "No doubt many acts of pillage, robbery and violence were committed by these bummers; for I have since heard of jewelry taken from women and the plunder of articles that never reached the commissary." But, he continued in his protest, "these acts were exceptional and incidental."

Sherman's own restraint was tested as the army's right wing, with which he was now riding, approached the town of Sandersville. Word came back that the advance guard had been fired upon from buildings and street corners. Assuming that the snipers were local citizens, Sherman vowed to burn the town in reprisal. It soon developed, however, that the riflemen had been members of Wheeler's cavalry corps. Sherman swiftly canceled his order; only the courthouse, which had been fortified, would be burned. "The General would be justified by laws of war," Henry Hitchcock wrote, "in destroying the whole town."

The army was plagued by other problems. What had begun as a joyous liberation of the slaves along the route increasingly became a nightmare. A huge train of blacks trailed after the marching columns — about 25,000 in all left the farms and plantations where they lived to follow the troops. Sherman urged them to stay home and await the War's end, and often exhorted black spokesmen, usually clergymen, to spread the word that the army could not afford to encumber its columns with so many noncombatants.

But nothing Sherman could say diminished the stream of liberated slaves. The urge for freedom was too strong to be denied. A 70th Indiana officer wrote his wife: "It was very touching to see the vast numbers of colored women following after us with babies in their arms, and little ones like our Anna clinging to their tattered skirts. One poor creature, while nobody was looking, hid two boys, five years old, in a wagon, intending, I suppose, that they should see the land of freedom if she couldn't."

As the army moved closer to Savannah, through country that grew ever more swampy, this situation led to tragedy. The streams of refugees were becoming more and more cumbersome. Officers dreaded the results should a real battle start. Finally General Davis' impatience with the refugee hordes crystallized into action. His corps was bringing up the rear of Slocum's left wing and represented the last chance of freedom for about 650 of the blacks, many of them women and children, who were following on its heels. Then Davis came to Ebeneezer Creek, a brown stream more than 100 feet wide. He hurried the 58th Indiana ahead to throw a pontoon bridge over the stream. Davis marched the troops across while the exslaves were held back under guard. As the men crossed the bridge many of the blacks worked forward to the water's edge, but guards kept them away from the span. When the last unit was over, the guards boarded the bridge, cut it loose from the shore and pulled themselves to the far bank, leaving the blacks stranded.

Chaplain John Hight of the 58th Indiana was watching. As the blacks realized they had been abandoned, he wrote, "there went up from that multitude a cry of agony." They looked back along the causeway into the dark swamp through which they had come: Wheeler's troopers were in there, for they had been following closely all day, and now the slaves' protectors were gone. The wail grew louder. There were shouts that Wheeler was there and those at the rear surged forward, thrusting those in front into the water. Watching from the far bank, Hight saw "a wild rush." Some of the people "plunged into the water and swam across. Others ran wildly up and down the banks, shaking with terror."

Almost immediately women and children were drowning. The canvas pontoons on the far side had already been collapsed for pack-

ing in wagons, but engineers, horrified at the disaster General Davis' stratagem was causing, hurled wood into the stream and felled several trees, which toppled into the water. Some of the blacks bound the logs into a small raft, then made a rope of blankets to haul the raft back and forth across the creek. It could carry no more than six people and frequently turned over, but scores of women and children rode it across. Many others, however — women with babies in arms, children cut loose from parents — disappeared in the swift brown water. Others, said Private Harrison Pendergast of the 2nd Minnesota, "huddled as close to the edge of the water as they could get, some crying, some praying, and all fearful that the rebels would come before they could get over."

Confederate cavalrymen appeared, fired several shots that increased the panic and then wheeled away. The crossing continued as the Federal soldiers marched away on the road to Savannah. A giant black man stood in the shallows hauling the raft back and forth until Wheeler's troopers rode up again, took the remaining slaves prisoner and started them on the cruel trip back to their owners. No one ever knew how many had drowned, but the number was considerable. "As soon as the character of the unthinking rush and panic was seen," a Federal soldier wrote, "all was done that could be done to save them from the water; but the loss of life was still great enough to prove that there were many ignorant, simple souls to whom it was literally preferable to die free men rather than to live slaves."

The tragedy at Ebeneezer Creek happened little more than 20 miles from Savannah. The army was nearing its goal. The men were as confident as ever, and they were

A column of newly liberated slaves trails behind Sherman's army — despite Sherman's unwillingness to be burdened with their care. "Thousands of these poor people left their humble homes," wrote one soldier, "and trudged along, with no idea of where they were going, except that they were on the highway from slavery to freedom."

amazingly healthy. Only 2 percent of the entire 62,000, including the wounded, had been declared unfit for duty during the nearly month-long trek. Lacking Confederates to fight, the troops held sham battles when they encamped at night; regiments flung blazing pine knots at each other through the darkness. But ahead of them lay difficult country crossed by the wide Savannah and Ogeechee Rivers and defended by an enemy force of unknown size behind works of unknown strength. The last segment of the great march loomed as the most trying. The Midwestern farmboys chatted noisily about how they would gorge themselves on oysters when they reached salt water. But they knew that a bloody assault might be necessary before they could get them.

To Cousin Mary Lizzie Work, Of New Washington, Indiana.

MARCHING THROUGH GEORGIA

SONG AND CHORUS,

In Honor of Maj. Gen. SHERMAN'S FAMOUS MARCH "from Atlanta to the Sea."

Words and Music by

HENRY CLAY WORK.

CHICAGO:

PUBLISHED BY ROOT & CADY, No. 95 CLARK STREET.

Entered according to Act of Congress, 1865, by Root & Cady, in the Clerk's Office of the District Court for the Northern District of Illinois.

To Glorify a Campaign

Sherman's campaign drew praise from many quarters, but perhaps no tribute was so memorable as Henry C. Work's patriotic song, "Marching through Georgia." A fervent abolitionist, Work filled his song with images that glorified Sherman's men and the Union cause. In one verse, loyal Unionists in the South burst into tears at the sight of the Stars and Stripes. In another, slaves send up a cheer as Sherman's men approach.

Work's melodramatic lyrics turned out to be a perfect mirror of Northern sentiment. "Marching through Georgia" grew hugely popular. It inspired the illustrations by artist Charles Copeland on the following pages. And the song's stirring martial rhythm made it one of the most enduring musical pieces of the era. Few who heard the rousing chorus ever forgot it:

Hurrah! Hurrah! We bring the Jubilee!
Hurrah! Hurrah! The flag that makes you free!
So we sang the chorus from Atlanta to the sea,
While we were marching through Georgia.

HENRY CLAY WORK

Bring the good old bu - gle, boys! we'll sing an - oth - er song —

Sing it with a spir - it that will start the world a - long — Sing it as we used to sing it,

fif - ty thou - sand strong, While we were march - ing through Geor - gia.

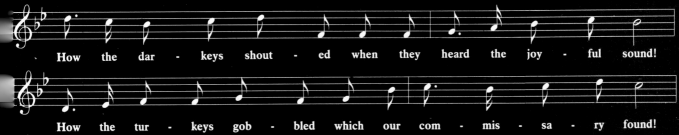

How the dar - keys shout - ed when they heard the joy - ful sound!

How the tur - keys gob - bled which our com - mis - sa - ry found!

Copeland '88

How the sweet po - ta - toes e - ven start - ed from the ground, While we were march - ing through Geor - gia.

Yes, and there were Un - ion men who wept with joy - ful tears,

When they saw the hon - or'd flag they had not seen' for years; Hard - ly could they be re - strained from

break - ing forth in cheers, While we were march - ing through Geor - gia.

So we made a thor - ough - fare for Free - dom and her train,

Six - ty miles in la - ti - tude — three hun - dred to the main; Trea - son fled be - fore us, for re -

sis - tance was in vain, While we were march - ing through Geor - gia.

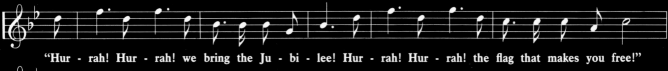

"Hur - rah! Hur - rah! we bring the Ju - bi - lee! Hur - rah! Hur - rah! the flag that makes you free!"

So we sang the chor - us from At - lan - ta to the sea, While we were march - ing through Geor - gia.

The Road to Tennessee

It was not until General Sherman and his four columns were well east of Atlanta that the Confederate army was ready to launch its counterinvasion of Tennessee. The Confederates and their commander, John Bell Hood, had reached Tuscumbia in the northwest corner of Alabama by November 1, intent on crossing the Tennessee River and striking north toward Nashville. But then had come three weeks of frustrating delays.

Hood decided that he must wait for Nathan Bedford Forrest and his 6,000 troopers to arrive to spearhead the advance. But Forrest was off on his raid on Johnsonville in central Tennessee. When Forrest's weary horsemen turned southward at last, they were bogged down by rain and mud and they did not reach Hood's camps until the middle of November. Then, badly needed supplies that should have arrived by rail from Corinth, Mississippi, were delayed because of damage to the Memphis & Charleston line. Finally, more fierce storms turned Hood's camps and routes of march into quagmires.

The postponements drove General P.G.T. Beauregard, Hood's superior, to frenzies of impatience. Hood's invasion plan had always depended for success on striking the Union forces in Tennessee before they were fully organized. Beauregard repeatedly urged Hood to get started, even if it meant doing so without Forrest's cavalry. But then Beauregard recalled Napoleon's maxim, Better one bad general than two good ones. On Novem-

ber 17 he left Hood to his own devices and headed east toward Macon, Georgia, in what would prove to be a vain attempt to help the Confederates there devise a plan for stopping Sherman's march.

Four more days passed before Hood at last started his army for Tennessee. Despite the delays, he still dreamed of the sort of lightning offensive that Stonewall Jackson had managed in the Shenandoah Valley. After smashing the Federals in middle Tennessee, Hood would drive on to Nashville, capture Union stores and recruit Southern sympathizers as he went. At the least, this campaign offensive would force Sherman to turn in pursuit, backtracking out of Georgia. At best, it might — or so Hood imagined — reverse the course of the War.

In fact, the Confederates' extended stay at Tuscumbia had lengthened the odds against them while yielding few benefits. Rations were still in short supply. Some troops were barefoot; most were clothed in tattered uniforms. And now winter was here. It was sleeting on the morning of November 21 as Hood's army set out from Florence on the north bank of the Tennessee River.

Still, the men were in remarkably good spirits. Many were natives of Tennessee and they were heading home. As one Tennessean wrote that first night, "The ground is frozen hard and a sharp, cold wind is blowing, but as my face is toward Tennessee, I heed none of these things." After crossing into Tennes-

This leather cartridge box was carried during Hood's Tennessee Campaign by Confederate infantryman C. D. Gant of the consolidated 3rd and 5th Missouri. Gant was wounded and taken prisoner at Franklin on November 30, 1864, during a desperate assault on the Federals entrenched there.

see, the men cheered as they were given a welcoming speech by Governor-in-exile Isham Harris, riding as an aide to Hood.

The troops were in an optimistic mood for another reason. Hood had implied that he would not fling them against strong, entrenched enemy forces as he had done in the past. The general had vowed, wrote Captain Samuel T. Foster of Granbury's Texas Brigade, "that we will have some hard marching and some fighting, but that he is not going to risk a chance for defeat in Tennessee. That he will not fight in Tennessee unless he has an equal number of men and choice of the ground." In short, the men would not be wasted in attacks that had little chance of success. Unfortunately for the Confederates, this was a promise Hood would not keep.

With Forrest and his cavalrymen riding ahead and covering the right flank, the Confederate infantry slogged northward in three columns. Farthest west, on the left, was a corps led by Major General Benjamin Franklin Cheatham, an experienced officer who had fought in most of the western war's roughest battles, including Shiloh, Stones River and Chickamauga.

On the right marched the corps under the command of Lieutenant General Alexander Stewart, also a veteran of virtually every battle in the west. Advancing between these two corps was the third, headed by Stephen Dill Lee, a West Pointer from North Carolina and the youngest lieutenant general in the Confederate Army.

After a march of about 70 miles, the three corps — 12 divisions in all — were to rendezvous at a village called Mount Pleasant. Reunited, they would form an army of 38,000 men, counting Forrest's cavalry, backed by 108 guns. This strong, compact force would

then move another dozen miles eastward to Columbia, a town of vital strategic importance. There the Franklin & Columbia Turnpike — the main road running north to Nashville — crossed the Duck River. On the turnpike 30 miles south of Columbia, at Pulaski, sat two Federal corps under the command of Major General John Schofield — roughly 30,000 men sent back from Atlanta by Sherman to help defend Tennessee.

Hood's purpose was simple: to seize Columbia and trap Schofield south of the Duck River, thus preventing him from joining the army being assembled by Major General George Thomas in Nashville. If Hood could get between the two armies with his force, which was larger than either, he could attack one and defeat it, then turn on the other. Such a brilliant double victory, as Hood saw it, would shatter all Federal opposition in Tennessee. The trick was to reach Columbia first, before Schofield could move.

Hood's long delay at Tuscumbia had been a boon to General Thomas. When Thomas had first arrived in Nashville late in September, he had found Federal detachments scattered all over southern Tennessee and northern Alabama: 5,000 men at Chattanooga, 5,000 at Murfreesboro, 4,000 at Decatur. Only about 10,000 troops plus quartermaster personnel defended his Nashville headquarters. Sherman had ordered two divisions to hurry east from Missouri, but they had been delayed.

Thomas busied himself pulling some of these units together while his small and poorly mounted cavalry force was being reorganized by a whip-cracking young brigadier general named James H. Wilson, who had most recently commanded a cavalry division

PRIVATE W. F. HENRY, 6TH TENNESSEE

PRIVATE THOMAS MURRELL, 6TH TENNESSEE

under General Philip Sheridan in the Army of the Shenandoah. While Thomas was involved in strengthening his position at Nashville, he left Schofield at Pulaski, about 75 miles to the south. Evidently Thomas thought that once Hood had begun his expected advance, Schofield would be able to hurry northward on the Columbia Pike to help repel the Confederates' invasion.

The force at Pulaski, made up of Schofield's own XXIII Corps and Major General David S. Stanley's IV Corps, was for the most part capably led. Stanley, who would win the Congressional Medal of Honor in the fighting to come, had been an effective cavalry leader before being promoted to command of an infantry division and then a

corps. The small army's division commanders were also experienced officers, especially Major General Jacob D. Cox, a former lawyer and politician from Ohio, and Brigadier General Thomas Wood, a West Point graduate and a hard fighter.

The least admired of the Federal officers at Pulaski was Schofield himself. A plump, ambitious man of 33, he felt that his career had not advanced with the speed his abilities deserved; he was known for trying to gain advantage by blackening the reputations of others with insidious complaints to Washington. Stanley detested him — after the War he would call him a liar and a fool. Schofield in turn habitually condemned General Thomas for excessive caution.

When Hood pushed north into Tennessee in late November of 1864, it was an exhilarating homecoming for the many natives of that state in his Army of Tennessee, including the two soldiers above, photographed early in the War. By the end of 1864, however, more than a third of Hood's force would be lost, and among the casualties would be Private Murrell (right), slain at Franklin.

In fact, it was Schofield who had a ready nose for danger — and by mid-November he was sniffing peril in the air. He had known Hood well at West Point and feared the impetuous Confederate general's penchant for swift attacks. Further, he felt himself in an exposed position at Pulaski.

It was fortunate for Schofield that he foresaw trouble. Alexander Stewart's Confederate corps had reached Lawrenceburg, 20 miles west of Pulaski and halfway to Columbia, before Federal cavalry scouts reported that Hood was on the move. Schofield immediately ordered his troops to break camp and head northward. By first light on November 22, his five divisions, 62 guns and 800 wagons were starting up the Columbia Turnpike, making as good time as rain and mud would allow. Schofield was in a life-and-death race, and he knew it.

The retreating Federal column was harassed at every turn by Forrest's indefatigable troopers, who were leading Stewart's advance. It fell to James Wilson's outnumbered horsemen to hold off the enemy riders until the Federal infantry could reach Columbia. Major Henry C. Connelly of the 14th Illinois Cavalry — part of Colonel Horace Capron's brigade — remembered watching the Federal rear guard give way under Confederate attack. As Forrest's horsemen thundered down on the brigade, Connelly warned Capron that the troopers "could not hold a moment against the troops pressing us in the rear and on the flanks."

Capron replied that he had been ordered to hold. Connelly cried, "We are destroyed and captured if we remain here." Capron reluctantly ordered his men back, but it was too late to avoid the Confederate charge. "Our command was confined to a narrow lane with men and horses in the highest state of excitement," Connelly recalled. Worse, the 14th Illinois had previously been taken prisoner and then paroled, and the men had been stripped of their fast-firing Burnside carbines. "We were armed with Springfield rifles," Connelly wrote, "which after the first volley were about as serviceable to a cavalryman thus hemmed in as a good club. The men could not reload while mounted, in the excitement of horses as well as soldiers. The only thing that could be done was to get out as promptly as possible."

This they did, but not without loss. In such delaying action, Capron's brigade was reduced from 1,200 men to about 800. The troopers' stubborn fighting, however, helped stall Forrest just long enough to allow General Cox and his 5,000-man division to reach Columbia by November 24. It was a hairbreadth affair. "In another hour Forrest would have been in possession of the crossings of Duck River," wrote Captain Henry Stone, one of General Thomas' aides temporarily assigned to Schofield's staff, "and the only line of communication with Nashville would have been in the hands of the enemy." Soon General Stanley and his IV Corps, having marched 30 miles nonstop, arrived to reinforce Cox. "These timely movements," Captain Stone summed up, "saved the little army from utter destruction."

As the Federal troops filed into Columbia, they set to work building an arc of trenches south of the town. Hood's three corps soon drew up, facing the Federal defenses. Now Schofield was in a dangerous position, with his back to the river. Worse, it was clear that the Confederates could easily throw a pontoon bridge across the Duck above or below the town and circle in the Federal rear. On

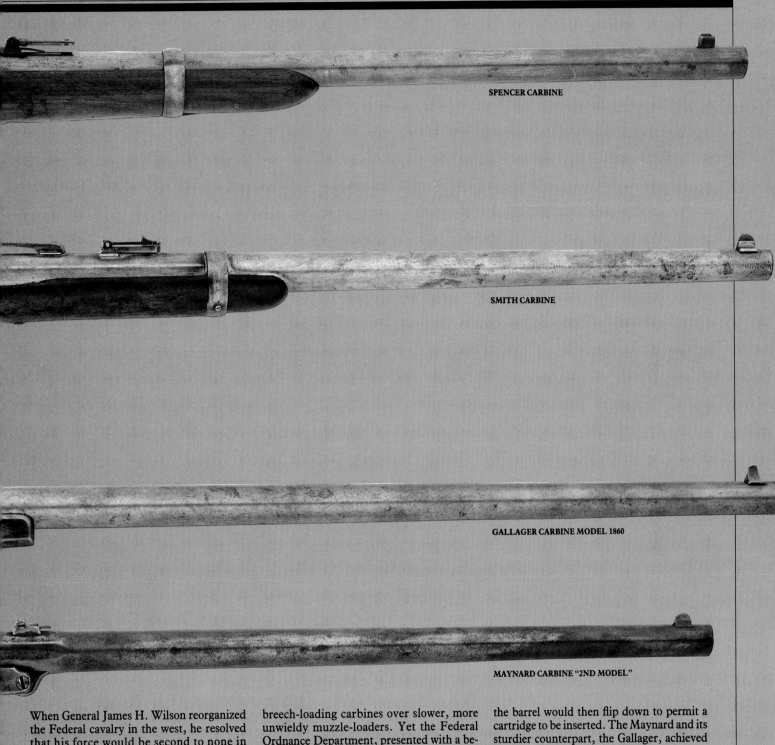

SPENCER CARBINE

SMITH CARBINE

GALLAGER CARBINE MODEL 1860

MAYNARD CARBINE "2ND MODEL"

When General James H. Wilson reorganized the Federal cavalry in the west, he resolved that his force would be second to none in firepower. His objective was symbolized by the cavalry emblem he chose: Above crossed sabers it bore the profile of a breech-loading Spencer carbine (top). This was no idle gesture. By early 1865 Wilson would have 13,000 troopers armed with the Spencers.

From the start of the War, cavalry officers were quick to recognize the advantages for horse soldiers of quick-firing, compact, breech-loading carbines over slower, more unwieldy muzzle-loaders. Yet the Federal Ordnance Department, presented with a bewildering array of carbines by Northern firms, had difficulty settling on one model. In the end, the demand proved so great that Washington took whatever it could get; more than 17 designs were in use during the War.

The models above exhibit various solutions to the problem of crafting a carbine for rear-loading. The Smith had a hinged breech released by a pushpin in front of the trigger; the barrel would then flip down to permit a cartridge to be inserted. The Maynard and its sturdier counterpart, the Gallager, achieved the same end with a hand lever; depressed, the lever moved the barrel forward from the breech so that it tipped down.

But none of these single-shot models could match the Spencer, which held seven cartridges in its magazine and could be reloaded with a flick of the lever. For its rapid-fire performance in Federal hands, it was touted as the gun that "ended the Civil War."

the night of November 27, Schofield drew his army back across the stream and destroyed Columbia's two bridges. The Confederates immediately occupied the town.

Snow was falling on frozen ground that night, but Hood was in "the best of health and spirits, and full of hope," according to Bishop Charles T. Quintard, chaplain of the 1st Tennessee. Hood had formulated a plan that he was sure would succeed. The next day Forrest would move upriver — eastward — and ford the Duck, clearing the way for the infantry. Cheatham's and Stewart's corps would follow, crossing a bridge to be laid at Davis' Ford, and aim for Spring Hill, a hamlet 12 miles north of Columbia on the turnpike. Thus "by a bold and rapid march," as Hood later wrote, the Confederate army would gain Schofield's rear "before he was fully apprised of my object." To hold Schofield in place, Stephen Lee would stay in Columbia with two of his three divisions and the bulk of the Confederate artillery, which would make a loud demonstration. Altogether it was a Stonewall Jackson-like scheme, Hood thought — "one of those interesting and beautiful moves upon the chessboard of war, to perform which I had often desired an opportunity."

Forrest's troopers forded the Duck on November 28, driving back the Union cavalry. That night Hood's chief engineer, Lieutenant Colonel Stephen W. Presstman, laid a pontoon bridge across the river. Well before dawn Cheatham's corps crossed unimpeded, followed by Stewart's. Hood was up by 3 a.m. to oversee the move, attended by Bishop Quintard, who called down God's blessing on the general and his men. "Thank you, doctor," said the pious Hood. "That is my hope and trust."

While Hood got his troops in motion, Schofield sat on the north bank of the Duck across from Columbia, fearful of what his foe might do but unwilling as yet to fall back. He ignored a message from General Wilson on the 28th reporting that Forrest's troopers were across the river east of town and driving back the Federal cavalry. Schofield had taken an immediate dislike to the energetic but quarrelsome Wilson and discounted the young cavalry general's warning that a full-scale crossing by Hood's infantry was likely. Schofield also ignored another message from Wilson, dispatched at 1 a.m. on November 29, that the Confederates had their pontoon bridge in place and that their vanguard might well reach Spring Hill via the turnpike by ten the same morning.

Major General Nathan Bedford Forrest, commander of Confederate cavalry during the Tennessee Campaign, combined sheer audacity with an innate cunning that baffled his adversaries. "He had never read a military book in his life," Sherman said later, "but he had a genius for strategy which was original, and to me incomprehensible."

Schofield finally stirred himself after dawn when yet another message arrived from Wilson, reporting more enemy movements. Alerting General Stanley, Schofield sent him with two divisions up the turnpike, with orders to post one of the divisions halfway to Spring Hill. Then, rather astonishingly, Schofield sent a brigade up the Duck River on a reconnaissance in force to see if what his own cavalry had reported was true.

Schofield refused, however, to move the rest of his force. Stephen Lee was keeping up a steady bombardment, which made the Union general suspect that he might be attacked where he was. If Confederate infantry were in fact crossing the Duck, they could easily come back down the river's north bank and assail his flank. So he waited on the

Brevet Major General James H. Wilson took charge of the Federal cavalry in Tennessee in November 1864 and was tested at once by the redoubtable Forrest. The rivalry would prove intense, for Wilson shared his counterpart's fondness for the bold stroke. "Cavalry is useless for defense," he once remarked. "Its only power is in a vigorous offensive."

heights overlooking Columbia — "just what his opponent wanted him to do," Wilson later growled.

Meanwhile, through the early hours of November 29, Hood was riding northward with Cheatham's corps, certain his chessboard maneuver was going as planned. Schofield was evidently still on the banks of the Duck — "I could distinctly hear the roar of Lee's artillery at Columbia," Hood later wrote — and Forrest's horsemen, having pushed the main body of Wilson's cavalry well to the north toward the town of Franklin, were closing in on Spring Hill. The infantry was marching in good order, unseen and unmolested, on a road heading north parallel to the Columbia Pike. Hood expected that lead elements would join the cavalry in Spring Hill by early afternoon, firmly closing Schofield's route of escape.

But a hitch in Hood's scheme soon developed. The energetic Stanley, hastening up the turnpike with Brigadier General George D. Wagner's division and all of the Federal reserve artillery, was already in striking distance of Spring Hill. Marching at the head of this column was a veteran brigade commanded by Colonel Emerson Opdycke, a 34-year-old Ohioan who was a natural soldier and a tough disciplinarian nonetheless popular for the care he took of his men.

As Opdycke and his brigade neared the village, they met a badly frightened Federal trooper who breathlessly reported that Forrest's horsemen, having swung wide around the town, were coming at a gallop from the north and east. Opdycke responded immediately. Taking his men into Spring Hill on the run, he deployed them quickly and drove back the initial assault by the Confederate cavalry, who were surprised to find more

Protected by earthworks, Federal infantry fire on Forrest's advancing cavalrymen near Spring Hill on the afternoon of November 29. "We charged through a beautiful grove, the men urging their horses," a Confederate recalled. "We had almost reached the edge of the woods when the shock came."

than a tiny garrison defending the place.

While Forrest's riders fell back to regroup, Stanley and Wagner hurried the rest of the division forward and placed their 34 guns on a rise south of the town. This was done "not a moment too soon," wrote Captain Stone, for the Confederates again attacked, charging from a quarter of a mile away straight at Opdycke's hastily established line. The enemy horsemen came on, recalled L. G. Bennett of the 36th Illinois,

"like waves angrily rolling upon a storm-washed beach."

But Opdycke's seasoned defenders held their fire until the attackers were near and then blasted them with repeated volleys, which were supported by fire from the Federal guns. "You could see a rebel's head falling off his horse on one side and his body on the other," reported a Wisconsin infantry-man. "Others you could see fall off with their feet caught in the stirrup, and the horse drag-

ging and trampling them, dead or alive.''
Again the Confederate troopers retreated,
now too battered and low on ammunition to
make another attack.

Given a respite, General Stanley arranged
his defenses, posting his three brigades—
about 5,000 men overall—in a semicircle
around Spring Hill. The troops immediately began dismantling fences to construct
their breastworks with the wooden rails. It

seemed clear that Hood's entire army was on
the move and meant to take the Spring Hill
crossroads. It was equally clear to Stanley
and his soldiers that they had to hold open
the escape route for the rest of the army.

A Confederate assault was not long in
coming. By 3 p.m., Cheatham's infantry
corps had almost reached Spring Hill, with
Major General Patrick Cleburne's famous,
hard-hitting division in the lead. Now the

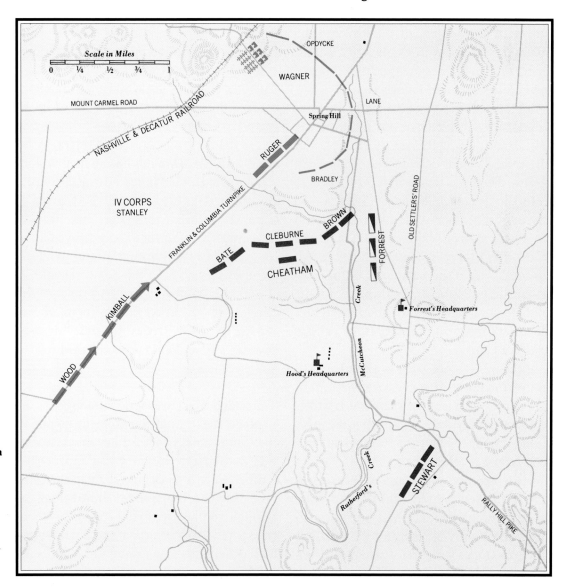

Around 7 p.m. on November 29,
Cheatham's Confederate corps and
Forrest's cavalry were arrayed just
south of Spring Hill, but Hood's
bid to cut off Schofield's Federals as
they withdrew northward on the
Franklin & Columbia Turnpike was in
jeopardy. During the afternoon Wagner's Union division, deployed in
an arc around Spring Hill, had beaten
back successive assaults, first by
Forrest's troopers and later by Cleburne's division. Now Hood was beset by darkness, difficult terrain
and confusion within his command —
and Federals were streaming up
the pike unhindered.

Confederates deployed into attack formation and moved forward. "I remember distinctly the beautiful day," wrote Captain W. O. Dodd, one of Forrest's officers. "The old rugged veterans of Cheatham's corps came marching up on our left with their battle flags waving in the mellow sunlight, and we felt that a long sought opportunity had at last arrived." Their numbers meant they must win: Cheatham's corps alone outnumbered Stanley's single division by at least 2 to 1. And with Stanley out of the way and the Columbia Turnpike in Confederate hands, Dodd wrote, "the surrender of Schofield would follow as night follows day."

But things began to go wrong for the Confederates. Cleburne's troops, making the first assault, evidently had no clear idea of where the Federal defense line was located because Forrest's cavalrymen had failed to scout the ground. Cleburne's men veered left, exposing their right flank to Federal fire, rather than attacking head on in proper order. The Federal defense bent, but it did not break. Then three batteries of the Federal artillery reserve opened up, raking the Confederate attackers with a murderous fire. Cleburne's troops dropped back to wait for reinforcements.

As the fresh troops arrived, Cheatham had his division under Major General William B. Bate deploy on Cleburne's left and instructed Major General John C. Brown to move his division behind Cleburne's battered infantry and prepare to renew the assault.

Again there was confusion. Afternoon was dwindling to winter twilight as the units shuffled into place, and it was near dark before Brown's division found its position. When his troops were ready to move, Brown discovered that the Federal lines were not where the Confederates thought. The attack as planned would not work. Brown sent for new orders but evidently received only vague instructions in reply.

In any event, Brown never launched his attack — and the other divisions were waiting for his assault before they would move. "I remember how anxiously we sat on our horses on a hillside overlooking the fertile fields around Spring Hill," Captain Dodd continued, "and expected, in vain, at least to see the battle. But alas! night came on and we went into camp." As the last moments of daylight slipped away, Hood's Confederates began to settle down for the night; cooking fires winked and then blazed in the frosty darkness.

The failure to attack rankled veterans ever afterward. "Had we not been halted and instead made a determined advance," wrote Brigadier General Daniel C. Govan of Cheatham's corps years later, "we could in 20 minutes have captured or destroyed Stanley." But, Govan wrote, "a fatal paralysis seemed to have seized those in command."

General Stanley remained proud of the role he had played on the afternoon of November 29, 1864. It was, he said, "the biggest day's work I ever accomplished for the United States."

The stalled attack was serious enough for the Confederates, but at the moment no one in that camp noticed something much worse. The Confederate infantry had approached Spring Hill at a 45-degree angle to the turnpike. Now the troops were camped along the hamlet's southeastern edge. Their bivouacs were parallel to the road — and did not cross it. The Federal escape route was still open.

Hood was unaware of this oversight when,

His sword drawn, Major General Benjamin F. Cheatham urges troops of his Confederate corps forward during the Tennessee Campaign. A powerfully built Tennessean given to outbursts of profanity, Cheatham *(portrait at right)* was incensed at Hood's assertion that he had failed to carry out his orders at Spring Hill.

having set up his headquarters at Absolam Thompson's house just below Spring Hill, he called a meeting of his officers. They were surprised to find that Hood seemed undisturbed by the failure of the attack and astounded to hear Hood declare that they would strike in the morning after a rest.

"I was never more astonished than when General Hood informed me that he had concluded to postpone the attack till daylight," Cheatham insisted later, perhaps in an attempt to shed blame for what followed. Others reported that Cheatham was distracted that night by the company of the charming Mrs. Jessie Peters. This vivacious woman had a dangerous attraction for Confederate generals; only the year before, her husband had shot and killed the indefatigably amorous General Earl Van Dorn in a jealous rage.

Sometime well after nightfall it seems to have occurred to Hood that the turnpike was still open. Apparently the thought did not alarm him, probably because he had convinced himself that Stephen Lee's bombardment would rivet Schofield indefinitely. At any rate, Hood's response was anything but forceful. First he asked General Stewart, who had just arrived with his corps, to put a

brigade across the Columbia Pike. Stewart said that his men were tired and hungry and that he would rather not disturb them. How about Forrest? The cavalryman was willing, as always, but two of his divisions were out of ammunition and the third had only a handful of cartridges taken from Federal prisoners.

At that Hood let the matter drop. It was late, and he may have needed to believe that all was well. He told General Bate that the turnpike north of Spring Hill was blocked by cavalry, "and so in the morning we will have a surrender without a fight. We can sleep quietly tonight."

But Schofield was awake. By midafternoon on November 29 he had recognized Hood's intention at last, and he immediately set out northward on a forced march, riding ahead with Brigadier General Thomas H. Ruger's division. Cox's division was to follow. By 7 p.m. — about the time Hood was conferring with his generals — Schofield and Ruger's lead brigade had already stolen past the Confederates camped along the turnpike and had reached Spring Hill.

There Schofield heard a dismaying report that Confederates were astride the pike three miles to the north at Thompson's Station.

He hurried on with Ruger's men — and discovered only the coals of recent campfires. One of Forrest's patrols had just decamped. Schofield then sent his chief engineer, Captain William J. Twining, galloping to Franklin with instructions to send a message to Thomas at Nashville. Schofield listened as hoofbeats drumming on frozen ground faded into the distance: That part of the turnpike, too, was still open. Soon Twining was wiring Schofield's report: "He regards his situation as extremely perilous."

The Federals strung out behind Schofield also felt in danger, marching up the turnpike within a stone's throw of Hood's army. "We were in such close proximity to the Confederates," wrote Captain James A. Sexton of the 72nd Illinois, "that we could see their long line of campfires as they burned brightly; could hear the rattle of their canteens; see the officers and men standing around the fires; while the rumbling of our wagon train on the pike, and the beating of our own hearts were the only sounds we could hear on our side."

Lieutenant Gus Smith of the 111th Ohio remembered that "a whispered word came down the line, 'It is Hood's whole army, and now we must try to steal by them.' We could have shot their men down while they sat by their campfires." The wooden bridges spanning the local streams "were covered with the blankets hastily taken from our knapsacks that the tread of our feet and the sound of the horses might not be heard by their outposts. We rapidly left the lights of their campfires behind us and heaved a sigh of relief as the last one disappeared from view."

One of the strangest and most daring escapes in the War's history was taking place, and of course it did not go entirely undetect-

Major General John Schofield was a keen and contentious officer who, like his former West Point classmate John Bell Hood, was sometimes on worse terms with his superiors than with the enemy. He was quick to criticize his commander, George Thomas, yet referred to Hood — his adversary at Spring Hill and Franklin — as a "jolly good fellow."

ed. Several Union regiments reported challenges from Confederate pickets and scattered exchanges of small-arms fire. But no Confederate force of any size moved to block the turnpike as most of two entire Federal corps and a five-mile-long wagon train moved past in the darkness.

Hood went to sleep at 11 p.m. Soon he was awakened to hear a report that Federal troops had been seen on the turnpike, but the news was hours old and there had been no confirmation. Sometime later a barefoot private appeared at headquarters on his own to report that the Yankees were moving.

Awakened again, Hood said to tell Cheatham, and once more he sought the warmth of his blankets.

Cheatham was pondering similar information from a staff officer, Captain Joseph Bostick, when the word from Hood arrived. Cheatham now sent Bostick to Major General Edward Johnson with orders to advance his division to the turnpike. General Johnson — "Old Clubby," who had been captured at Spotsylvania in May and then exchanged and sent west — greeted the order with a display of his celebrated temper. His division was part of Stephen Lee's corps temporarily attached to Cheatham, and he resented taking orders from a strange commander — especially in the middle of the night. He "commenced complaining bitterly that he had been 'loaned out,' " Cheatham later wrote. And then Johnson demanded of Bostick to know why General Cheatham did not order out one of his own divisions.

Despite his choleric outburst, Johnson stirred himself and rode away to the turnpike with Bostick — only to find the road empty. How he missed the marching Federals remains unclear; perhaps there was a gap between units.

Through much of the night Ruger's, Cox's and Nathan Kimball's divisions continued their march past the Confederates and on beyond Spring Hill. Well before dawn Stanley's troops, now bringing up the rear, had cleared the village, and by early morning on November 30 the small Federal army was intact eight miles to the north in Franklin. Thus Schofield had escaped. But it had been close. A single Confederate brigade "planted squarely across the pike," as Captain Stone put it, "either south or north of Spring Hill, would have effectually prevent-ed Schofield's retreat, and daylight would have found his whole force cut off from every avenue of escape by more than twice its numbers, to assault whom would have been madness, and to avoid whom would have been impossible."

When Hood awakened to find that the Federals had eluded his troops, he was as "wrathy as a rattlesnake," according to General John Brown. Breakfast that morning, to which Hood summoned Brown and all of his other chief subordinates, was an unseemly affair marked by shouted recriminations and heated denials. Men white with anger accused each other, uttered threats, demanded apologies. Hood scorched them all for, as he put it, ruining "the best move in my career as a soldier." His chief blame fell on Cheatham, who vehemently denied the charge.

At no time did Hood condemn himself in any way for the debacle. It was not his own negligence or confusion — or even plain mishap — that had let the Federals escape. As he ruminated on the wrongs done him, he decided ultimately that not only his generals but also his men were at fault. They had, he said, lost their courage. He had not crushed Stanley the previous afternoon because, very simply, his troops were afraid to fight.

This was a theme that Hood had harped on in the past. As he saw it, the army's previous commander, Joseph Johnston, had softened the men during the summer when he had retreated all the way from Chattanooga to Atlanta. According to Hood, the troops were "still, seemingly, unwilling to accept battle unless under the protection of breastworks." As before, when he had assumed command of the army from Johnston in front of Atlanta, Hood decided that the only cure for such cowardice was to throw his troops into battle. Such attacks had been disastrous at Atlanta, and they would prove so again.

The Confederate army's morale, already depressed by the failure at Columbia, plummeted further. "I have never seen more intense rage and profound disgust than was expressed by the weary, footsore, battle-torn Confederate soldiers when they discovered that their officers had allowed the prey to escape," recalled Captain Dodd. "There was not an officer or private present who could but understand that a culpable and inexcusable blunder had been made," echoed General Govan.

Despite their anger and misgivings, the Confederate officers and men quickly broke camp, obeying Hood's orders to pursue the enemy up the Columbia Pike toward Franklin. In the lead was Patrick Cleburne's division of Cheatham's corps. Born in Ireland, Cleburne had migrated to America as a young man, settling in Helena, Arkansas. He organized a rifle company when the War began and went on to prove himself a remarkable soldier in battle after battle. Although he was known as "the Stonewall Jackson of the West" and his men admired him passionately, Confederate politics had blocked his advance to corps or army command and he remained a division head under men less competent than he.

As the long war wore on, a romantic strain in Cleburne's personality became evident. His adjutant, Captain Irving A. Buck, noticed it particularly as they neared Spring Hill on the 29th. They paused in the village of Ashwood, where "the beautiful little Episcopal church was in the purest Gothic style, its walls and sharp-pointed roof concealed by ivy, while the flowers and shrubbery looked fresh and green even on this bleak November

day." Cleburne had reined in his horse, Buck recalled, and stopping a moment to admire the place had murmured "that it was 'almost worth dying for, to be buried in such a beautiful spot.'"

At Franklin, while the Confederates hastened in pursuit, Schofield surveyed his options. He did not like what he saw. The town was tucked in a tight bend of the Harpeth River on the south bank — an awkward place, as he saw it, to make a stand. He itched to get his forces on the move again, to hurry them the final 18 miles to Nashville and a union with the troops of General Thomas. But Schofield feared that he would not be able to get his wagon trains across the Harpeth before Hood's army got there. The two bridges at Franklin were damaged and unusable; Schofield deemed the river unfordable, and he had scuttled his pontoons on leaving Columbia to lighten his train for the forced march north. The commander had asked Thomas to send a pontoon bridge to Franklin, but he now discovered to his dismay that none had yet arrived.

The situation shook Schofield, who was worn out in body and mind by the struggles of the past week. "In all my intimate acquaintance with him," General Jacob Cox wrote, "I never saw him so manifestly disturbed as he was in the glimmering dawn of that morning." There seemed to be nothing to do for the moment but stand and fight, so Schofield ordered Cox to have the two divisions of Schofield's own XXIII Corps dig in astride the turnpike, then to deploy one IV Corps division on the right flank. Cox was to "hold Hood back at all hazards till we can get our trains over, and fight with the river in front of us."

A view of Winstead Hill, looking south from the position held by General Wagner's Union division, surveys the open field traversed by the attacking Confederate infantrymen on November 30. "Very few battlefields of the war were so free from obstruction to the view," one of the Federal defenders remarked.

Cox, examining the ground, was delighted to discover that he could not have asked for a better position to defend. The handsome brick house he had chosen for his headquarters, owned by a farmer named Fountain Branch Carter, stood at the high point of a wide, almost treeless and slightly undulating plain. If Hood attacked, he would have to cross almost two miles of open ground, extending from a low ridge to the south known as Winstead Hill.

Using the Carter house and its cotton gin as a central point, Cox stretched his line in an arc anchored on the Harpeth below and above the town, and enclosing the tight bend in the river. The men, despite their fatigue, were soon busy digging. "After a short rest and some refreshments (including a ration of whiskey)," recalled Captain Sexton of the 72nd Illinois, "we went to work with a will, digging rifle pits and building entrenchments, and were thus engaged when we could distinguish skirmish firing in the distance, and see the ever present and everlasting wagon train coming in on the run."

While the troops worked, Schofield shook off his alarm and fatigue to make further defensive dispositions. Having discovered that the Harpeth was fordable after all, he crossed a dozen of his guns and posted them on the far side of the river in a redoubt called Fort Granger, built a year before to protect Franklin's two bridges. He also instructed General Thomas Wood's division of IV Corps to ford the river and protect the wagon train when it crossed. James Wilson's cavalry, meanwhile, scouted along the north bank, ready to delay the Confederates should they bypass Franklin and cross the river to fall on Schofield's rear. And the engineers got busy rebuilding the two half-destroyed bridges so the wagons could cross.

Gradually Schofield began to breathe more easily. By nightfall all his wagons would be on the north bank and he would be ready to put his men on the pike to Nashville—assuming, of course, that Hood did not attack him first. The Confederates were now close. The Federal rear guard, made up of General Wagner's division with Colonel

Opdycke's brigade covering, was giving ground but retiring in good order. When Hood reached the south side of Winstead Hill about 2 p.m., Wagner's regimental flags already dotted its slope. Hood sent Stewart's corps forward to flank the hill and force the Federals off it, then rode up for a look.

For a long time he studied the Federal lines through his field glasses, standing on his crutches under a tree. Forrest, who was with him, counseled against a head-on attack. He had fought here before and knew the strength of the Union position. But he thought Schofield's flanks vulnerable. "Give me one strong division of infantry with my cavalry," he said, "and within two hours I can flank the Federals from their works." Hood refused. He was determined to smash the Federal lines in a frontal assault.

General Cheatham found the prospects appalling. "I do not like the looks of this fight; the enemy has an excellent position and is well fortified."

"I prefer to fight them here," Hood snapped. He remarked that the Federals here had had only a few hours to build defenses, whereas at Nashville "they have been strengthening themselves for three years."

Cleburne, already criticized for supposedly not pressing hard enough at Spring Hill, declined to counsel against an attack. He rested his field glasses on a stump and studied the enemy line, murmuring at last, "They are very formidable." He wrote briefly in a small notebook, sitting on the stump.

At last Hood closed his glasses, cased them and turned to his officers. "We will make the fight," he said.

At his headquarters in a nearby house Hood outlined his plans. They were murderously simple. Without waiting for Stephen Lee's corps or for most of his artillery, which was still hours away on the road from Columbia, he would hurl Cheatham's and Stewart's men at the Federal trenches. What was more, the main attack would be made directly up the turnpike, striking the middle of the enemy line, although it was evident that this was the Federals' strongest point. It would be a headlong assault in the old manner — and it would restore the nerve, as Hood saw it, of his jaded troops. He had always associated valor with heavy casualties, even questioning the courage of subordinates who had kept their losses down. Now he would force his men into a bloodbath for their own good as an army.

So deep was this conviction — and so intense his rage over Spring Hill — that Hood did not bother to deploy his troops effectively for what was already a risky assault. The principal thrust up the turnpike would be made by only seven of the 18 brigades Hood had at his disposal: the three in Cleburne's division, the four in John C. Brown's.

Brown, who would move up the west side of the pike, put two brigades — under Brigadier Generals States Rights Gist and George Washington Gordon — in his front line. The two others, commanded by Brigadier Generals John C. Carter and Otho F. Strahl, would form a second line. Cleburne, who had a wider front to cover on the right side of the pike, was forced to spread out his three brigades in a single line: Hiram Granbury's Texans on the left, Daniel Govan's troops in the center and Mark Lowrey's on the right.

The other division in Cheatham's corps — three brigades under General Bate — was sent off to the left to make an attack in conjunction with a division of Forrest's cavalry. On the far right, Stewart's corps was de-

War on the Doorstep

Late on the afternoon of November 30, as the Confederate vanguard surged over the Federal breastworks at Franklin, a 67-year-old Tennessee planter by the name of Fountain Branch Carter found himself in the thick of the battle. Earlier that day Federal officers had commandeered part of his home (*below*), situated just 90 yards behind their main defense line; now Carter lay huddled with family members in the cellar as bullets rained against the brick walls above.

For Carter, the worst was yet to come: He would learn the next morning that his own son, Confederate Captain Theodoric "Tod" Carter, an aide in Cheatham's corps, had been gravely wounded in the assault. The elder Carter and his daughters were with the party that went in search of the boy and bore him back to the family's debris-strewn sitting room, where he died the following day. He had fallen within sight of the house — his first glimpse of home in more than two years.

FOUNTAIN BRANCH CARTER

CAPTAIN THEODORIC CARTER

ployed with its right flank on the river. Forrest and two of his divisions would attempt to drive back Wilson's Federal horsemen north of the river.

At this point the two armies were probably evenly matched, since Hood had denied himself the use of one of his three corps and virtually all of his artillery. But numbers were less important than the terrain — those two miles of open ground the Confederates would have to cross, unprotected by even a fence or an occasional stand of trees.

Hood would later avow that Cleburne had supported the plan of attack with high enthusiasm, but the Irishman's brigade commander and friend, Govan, a fellow Arkansan, remembered that "General Cleburne seemed to be more despondent than I ever saw him. I was the last one to receive any instructions from him and as I saluted and bade him goodby I remarked, 'Well, general, there will not be many of us that will get back to Arkansas,' and he replied, 'Well, Govan, if we are to die, let us die like men.' "

All that morning General Cox had been refining the Federal position. One weakness was the point where the Columbia Turnpike ran through the Federal trenches; here a gap in the breastworks had been purposely left open to allow the last of the artillery and wagons, as well as the men of Wagner's rear guard, to pass through. To protect the gap, Cox posted four guns at the opening. Then he had a second trench line dug 200 feet to the rear across the road. On both sides of the turnpike the main line angled back in gradual steps, conforming to the perimeter of the town. A second line protecting the turnpike angled back similarly on higher ground, and here more artillery was deployed to fire over

the first line and sweep the field in front.

By midafternoon Cox had done what he could, and he took a few moments to rest and survey the scene, as did his men. Many had eaten and some were dozing. "Our horses were fed and saddled and the orderlies lounged on the grass," Cox recalled, "while the officers were sitting on the veranda, smoking or sleeping as the mood took them. The day had proved to be a bright and warm one, a good example of Indian summer." Except for an occasional straggler, Cox wrote, "nothing was to be seen between us and the Winstead Hill two miles away."

But despite the atmosphere of calm readiness, the Federal dispositions were flawed in one crucial way. The mistake was made after George Wagner's division — the Federal rear guard — abandoned Winstead Hill in response to Stewart's flanking move. As his three retreating brigades neared the main Federal works, Wagner received an order — perhaps from Schofield, although the record is unclear — directing him to halt his troops astride the turnpike about half a mile out. Wagner was to remain there, or so several postbattle accounts maintained, only until Hood showed signs of advancing in force. Then he was to retreat inside the trench line, forming a reserve near the Carter house and its big cotton gin.

Wagner, it seems, took his orders to mean that he was to hold his exposed forward position no matter what. Colonel Opdycke, whose brigade was bringing up the rear of Wagner's division, apparently objected to this. According to witnesses, he declared that troops stationed in front of the main breastworks were in a position to aid the enemy — and no one else. Adding that his men were utterly worn out and needed relief, Op-

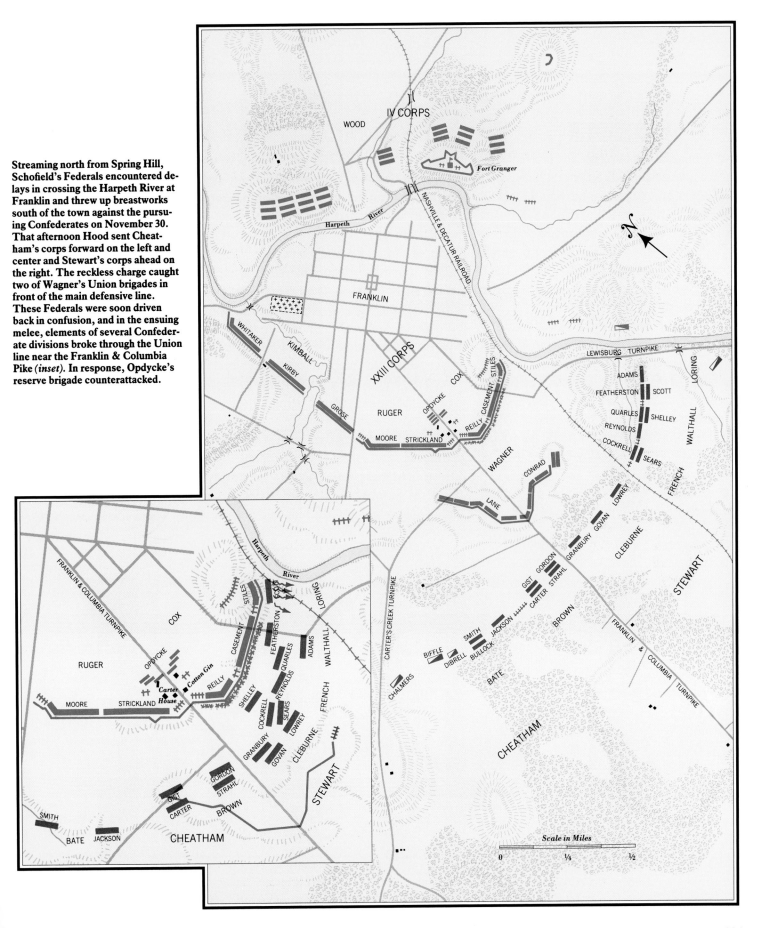

Streaming north from Spring Hill, Schofield's Federals encountered delays in crossing the Harpeth River at Franklin and threw up breastworks south of the town against the pursuing Confederates on November 30. That afternoon Hood sent Cheatham's corps forward on the left and center and Stewart's corps ahead on the right. The reckless charge caught two of Wagner's Union brigades in front of the main defensive line. These Federals were soon driven back in confusion, and in the ensuing melee, elements of several Confederate divisions broke through the Union line near the Franklin & Columbia Pike (*inset*). In response, Opdycke's reserve brigade counterattacked.

dycke marched his brigade the last half mile up the pike and into the Federal lines.

Wagner stayed where he was, however, placing his other two brigades on opposite sides of the turnpike and ordering them to scratch hasty entrenchments in the earth. And there they would remain, fatally exposed, until Hood's advancing troops were upon them.

A bare half hour before sunset, Hood's regiments in their yellowish brown "butternut" uniforms began their advance, marching onto the plain in battle order. The Federal soldiers watched transfixed as the low sun burnished the enemy bayonets and the Confederate bands played "The Bonnie Blue Flag" and "Dixie." Recalled Cox, "No more magnificent spectacle was ever witnessed." Rabbits bounded ahead of the advancing Confederate lines. Quail coveys burst up-

ward, wrote Captain Henry A. Castle of the 137th Illinois, and "flew off to the gray sky-light of the north" while the Confederates came on with "their red, tattered flags as numerous as though every company bore them, flaring in the sun's rays."

The attacking brigades marched to within a mile of the Federal lines, then paused before beginning their charge. The men waited quietly. General Cleburne marked out squares on the soft ground and began a game of checkers with leaves of different colors. A few of the troops ate all the rations they carried, in the expectation of being killed.

The bands struck up again as a skirmish line started out. Soon the entire army was on the move. "I was right guide to the 41st Tennessee, marching four paces to the front," Sergeant Samuel A. Cunningham wrote, "and I well remember the look of determina-

The Confederate breakthrough on the 30th led to furious fighting around the Carter cotton gin and shed seen here — situated just 50 feet north of the main Union line. A Federal infantryman who defended this ground recalled the enemy's approach: "It looked to me as though the whole South had come up there and were determined to walk right over us."

tion that was on every face. We went down the hill, across the brook, up the slope, over the railroad," recalled Cunningham; "then came the first deadly Yankee greeting—a shrapnel bursting in the ranks of Company E, killing and wounding nine men."

As the Confederates neared, panic began to build in the two Federal brigades Wagner was holding all alone 470 yards to the front. Everyone in the Federal main line expected Wagner's men to fall back when a direct attack came, but there they stood, their flanks in the air and about to be overlapped.

Several Federal officers galloped to Wagner's command post, warning him to move his men. "The orders are not to stand except against cavalry and skirmishers," one shouted. But Wagner, perhaps confused, perhaps thirsting for glory, refused to order his men back. Striking the ground with his walking stick, he replied, "Never mind; fight them."

Wagner's troops, veterans and new recruits alike, knew that a disastrous blunder was occurring. "The indignation of the men grew almost into a mutiny," recalled Captain John Shellenberger of the 64th Ohio, "and the swearing of those gifted in pro-

fanity exceeded all their previous efforts."

The Confederates were close now. From the main Federal line, Captain James Sexton of the 72nd Illinois saw their "swinging motion, noticeable when great bodies of men move together." Then the enemy troops paused, redressed their lines and charged. Recalled Captain Stone: "With that wild rebel yell which once heard is never forgotten, the great human wave swept along and seemed to engulf the little force that so sturdily awaited it."

At last Wagner's subordinate officers gave the order to fire, and a heavy volley crashed up and down the line. Some Confederates fell but the others picked up speed, screaming as they dashed forward. This was too much for Wagner's brigades; the troops broke, streaming back toward the Federal breastworks. Scores were shot as they ran, and nearly 700 were taken prisoner.

It quickly became evident that Wagner's foolhardy stand had placed the entire Federal army in jeopardy. The gunners and riflemen in the center of the main line were not able to fire at Cleburne's and Brown's attacking troops without running the risk of hitting their own retreating men. The Confederates immediately saw this, too. "The shout was raised, 'Go into the works with them!' " recalled General George Gordon, and the Confederates charged forward right on the heels of Wagner's troops. Many of Wagner's fleeing men became entangled in an abatis of felled locust trees in front of the Federal earthworks. The Confederate attackers shot, bayoneted or clubbed the trapped soldiers through the brush.

At last the surviving fugitives, most of them veering toward the gap in the earthworks at the turnpike, staggered to safety

103

In a postwar illustration of the Battle of Franklin, Union troops atop their defensive works meet the Confederates at point-blank range as Federal wagons cross the Harpeth River beyond. A lieutenant with the 12th Kentucky on the Federal left described the critical moment: "The struggle was across and over the breastworks. The standards of both armies were upon them at the same time."

inside the Union lines. Given a clear field of fire, the Federal infantry and artillery opened up with a roar. But it was too late to halt the oncoming Confederates who, Major S. L. Coulter of the 65th Ohio remembered, "continued to advance in a solid body, with their hats drawn down over their eyes, just as if advancing against a hailstorm."

A raw Federal regiment — the 104th Ohio — happened to be deployed at the gap, and among those men a panic was kindled. Captain Stone reported that the "tremendous onset, the wild yells, the whole infernal din of the strife, were too much for such an undisciplined body. As they saw their comrades from the advance line rushing to the rear, they too turned and fled. The contagion spread and in a few minutes a disorderly stream was pouring down the pike past the Carter house toward the town. The guns, posted on each side of the pike, were abandoned, and the works, for the space of more than a regimental front, both east and west of the pike, were deserted. Into the gap thus made without an instant's delay swarmed the jubilant Confederates, urged on by Cleburne and Brown, and took possession of both works and guns."

Thus the powerful Federal line was broken at its strongest point. The river crossings, so crucial to the survival of the Federal army, were now in danger of being seized. The unthinkable had happened, and the Confederates seemed poised on the edge of an incredible victory. Could Hood's dream of taking Nashville, roaring on beyond to the Ohio River and reversing the War in a stroke have substance after all? For now his men seemed unstoppable.

The Crude Fight against Disease

Of the 620,000 men who lost their lives in the Civil War, more than 60 percent died of disease. It was small wonder. The role of bacteria in disease was not yet understood, and antibiotics had not yet been discovered. Doctors and pharmacists knew little more about the use of drugs than their counterparts did in ancient times. The theories of healing that prevailed focused on controlling the bowels, the kidneys and the blood; the administration of cathartics, emetics and diuretics was a favorite treatment. Federal Surgeon General William A. Hammond *(below, right)* saved untold lives when he banned calomel and tartar emetic in 1863. Those popular medicines not only washed away vital fluids but also caused mercury poisoning.

Fortunately, however, most drugs were harmless and a few turned out to be extremely effective — particularly quinine, opium and the anesthetic chloroform. Quinine, produced from the bark of the South American cinchona tree, was used to treat malaria, just as it is today (even though that mosquito-borne disease was attributed to "stagnant water miasmas."). Quinine was also administered, usually with a shot of whiskey, for other ailments, including coughs, headaches, toothaches, syphilis and fevers. Opium, derived from Asiatic poppies, proved a potent though addictive painkiller in pill form, in tincture (laudanum) or as morphine. As a camphorated tincture (paregoric), opium was also used to control diarrhea.

This cast-iron mortar and pestle was used by William Whitlow, doctor of the Campbell County, Virginia, home guard. Denied raw materials and foreign-made drugs by the blockade, Southern doctors concocted remedies from such plants as pokeweed and sassafras.

Confederate Surgeon General Samuel P. Moore *(left)* and his Federal counterpart, William A. Hammond *(above)*, encouraged their governments to establish laboratories to test and manufacture drugs. Hammond's autocratic style eventually brought him into conflict with Secretary of War Edwin Stanton, who dismissed him in 1864.

CEPHAELIC IPECACUANHA (BRAZIL)

CINCHONA CORDIFOLIA (PERU)

PAPAVER SOMNIFERUM (ASIA)

These foreign-grown plants, identified by their botanical name and main country of origin, provided the raw materials for six widely used Civil War drugs *(clockwise from the top):* ipecac, used to induce vomiting; opium, the painkiller; rhubarb, a mild cathartic; jalap, a stronger cathartic; squill, used in small doses as an expectorant, in large doses as a diuretic and purgative; quinine, for malaria and general fevers.

SCILLA MARITIMA (MEDITERRANEAN SEACOAST)

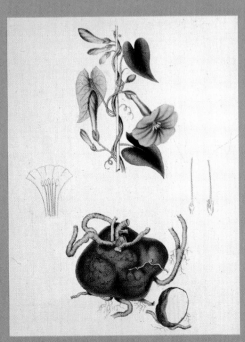

IPOMAE JALAP (SOUTH AMERICA)

RHEUM PALMATUM (CHINA, RUSSIA)

107

Producing Remedies for the Troops

The Union enjoyed an enormous advantage over the agrarian Confederacy in providing drugs for its armies. All the major pharmaceutical manufacturers were located in the Union, and in 1863 Surgeon General William A. Hammond set up two large government-operated laboratories at Astoria, New York, and Philadelphia, Pennsylvania, to augment drug production. The Philadelphia Laboratory turned out 48 types of medicine, including extracts, tinctures, powders, pills and salts. In addition, a filling department packed or bottled acids, gums, liquors, wines and oils bought from outside suppliers; a sewing department made sheets, pillowcases, towels, curtains and hospital clothes. At peak strength, the laboratory employed 350 female workers, along with skilled chemists.

The South, however, had only a few small government-run laboratories and lacked the chemicals and raw materials to adequately supply these facilities. Surgeon General Samuel P. Moore urged citizens to raise medicinal plants, such as flax, castor-oil beans and mustard, and even dispensed domestic poppy seeds in hopes that a gardener might derive an opium substitute. Doctors were given a list of 410 native wild plants with therapeutic value and urged to search for them in the fields and forests. The drug substitutes were generally better than nothing, although many, such as bugleweed when used for digitalis, proved worthless. A particular favorite with the soldiers was a quinine substitute they dubbed "old indigenous." It consisted of dried dogwood, poplar and willow bark — and a healthy dose of whiskey.

Two sentries guard the main building of the U.S. Army Laboratory at Philadelphia where German-born chemist John M. Maisch (*left*) supervised the testing and manufacturing of drugs. Maisch recruited many talented chemists; he shared with them the latest findings from German scientific journals.

With a pill-rolling machine like this one, a single operator at the Philadelphia factory could produce from 5,000 to 7,000 pills per day.

108

This 10-gallon copper percolator was of the type used at the Philadelphia Laboratory to extract the active ingredients of roots and bark. For large batches, the laboratory had 200-gallon percolators.

This bottle was filled at the Philadelphia Laboratory with quinine pills bought from a private firm. The number *34* on the label refers to the bottle's position in a field medicine kit.

"Crow's foot" scales such as the one shown here were employed at the laboratory to weigh substances up to about 40 pounds. Although sets of weights were made in the United States, the most accurate ones were imported from Europe.

Tools of the Healing Trade

Suppositories to treat diarrhea and piles were made in metal molds like this. The medicinal ingredient, usually powdered opium, tannic acid or lead acetate, was mixed with cocoa butter and whale-oil derivatives.

This 5-inch-long syringe, made of hard rubber, was used to apply medicated solutions and ointments as well as to wash out eyes and to irrigate wounds.

This spatula-like iron was used to spread resinous material containing drugs onto muslin, linen or chamois for application as plasters. Asafetida was used for coughs, belladonna and opium for rheumatism and neuralgia.

Field surgeons carried their medicine bottles and jars in leather kits like the one pictured here. Bandages, scissors, thread and other equipment were stored in the top of the kit, beneath the divider listing the contents.

A stand-in, garbed in the full-dress uniform of a hospital steward, poses with prescription ingredients and instruments in this U.S. Army Quartermaster Corps photograph taken in 1866. Stewards helped the field surgeons, kept medical records, supervised cooks and nurses and, in emergencies, prescribed drugs and performed minor surgery.

Small amounts of drugs were weighed with hand-held prescription scales. The scales were accurate, easy to use and inexpensive.

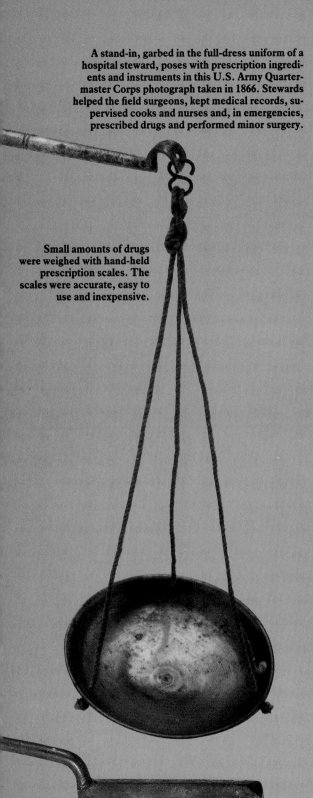

The patent medicines shown here are but a few of the dubious nostrums peddled to soldiers who preferred to treat themselves rather than entrust their ailments to Army doctors. Soldiers represented a vast market, and many dealers pitched their advertising toward them; one firm selling a purported cure for "camp itch" opened a sales office in Nashville after the Federals occupied that city.

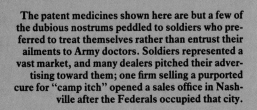

111

Missed Chance At Franklin

"I never saw the dead lay near so thick. I saw them upon each other, dead and ghastly in the powder-dimmed starlight."

COLONEL EMERSON OPDYCKE, U.S.A., AFTER THE BATTLE OF FRANKLIN

The Confederates at Franklin were winded by their long charge into the Federal breastworks, and the wild excitement of their unexpected success threw some of the units into confusion. But their position seemed brilliant. Three Confederate divisions led by Generals Cleburne, Brown and French had converged on the gaping hole torn in the Union line when George Wagner's Federal brigades had stampeded rearward. If the Confederates could maintain their headlong drive, they would widen the gap — and possibly destroy Major General John Schofield's entire Federal army.

The only man in a position to prevent the breakthrough was Colonel Emerson Opdycke, the strong-minded Ohio officer who had marched his brigade inside the Union lines an hour earlier, refusing to remain in the exposed position occupied by Wagner. Having gotten his weary troops to safety, Opdycke — who would come out of this day a brigadier general — had placed them in the first open spot he saw. This was a meadow about 200 yards behind the Carter house and just east of where the dangerous hole would be torn in the Union line.

Opdycke's men, their weapons stacked and coffeepots bubbling over small fires, were eating and resting around 4 p.m. when the noise of battle grew louder. Opdycke immediately ordered them to form in line. The troops had hardly grabbed their rifles before, in Opdycke's words, "a most horrible stampede of our front line troops came surging and rushing back past Carter's house." On their heels came the Confederates.

Opdycke shouted, "First Brigade, forward to the works!" and his men surged past the Carter house and directly into the gap in the Federal defenses. Just at that moment General Stanley, Opdycke's corps commander, arrived on the scene. "I saw Opdycke near the center of his line urging his men forward," Stanley recalled. "I gave the Colonel no orders as I saw him engaged in doing the very thing to save us, to get position of our line again." As Stanley rode forward to offer what help he could, his horse was shot from under him and a musket ball passed through the back of his neck, knocking him out of action.

Opdycke's brigade gathered up reinforcements as it rushed ahead. Two Kentucky regiments and the remnants of Wagner's other two brigades joined the charge. Yelling, weapons held high, the Federals crashed into the oncoming Confederates, beginning one of the most savage hand-to-hand struggles of the entire War.

"Some fought with entrenching tools," wrote Major S. L. Coulter. "The bayonet was freely used while others clubbed their guns and knocked each other's brains out." A Confederate soldier, recalled an Illinois officer, "thrust one of our men through with the bayonet, and before he could draw his weapon from the ghastly wound, his brains were scattered on all of us that stood near by the butt of a musket swung with

Men of the 12th U.S. Colored Troops fought bravely at Nashville under this banner, which depicts a recruit crushing the Serpent of Rebellion underfoot as Liberty bears aloft a Phrygian cap, granted to freed slaves in ancient Rome. When the 12th was forced to give ground at Nashville, Private Elijah Steel seized this flag and, in the words of his captain, held it "alone in the open field, in spite of the murderous fire of the enemy, until called by his officers to return."

terrific force by some big fellow whom I could not recognize in the grim dirt and smoke that enveloped us."

When the combatants had a chance to fire their weapons, it was at point-blank range. "One rebel," wrote Stuart F. Hoskinson of the 73rd Illinois, "was on the works above the head of one of our men and, I suppose, having fired his gun, had raised it in the act of clubbing the man below. I quickly brought my gun to bear on him and fired, and the last I saw of him he was falling backward with his hands in the air." The Illinois officer, Captain James A. Sexton, remembered discharging his weapon "nine times and the most distant man I shot at was not more than 20 feet away." Colonel Opdycke himself was seen "firing all the shots in his revolver and then breaking it over the head of a rebel."

Captain Sexton also recalled that a Confederate colonel jumped up on the breastworks and shouted at the Federals to surrender. "Private Arbridge of Company D, 72nd Illinois, thrust his musket against the abdomen of the rash colonel, and with the exclamation, 'I guess not!' instantly discharged his weapon. The effect of the shot was horrible and actually let daylight through the victim. The doomed warrior doubled up, his head gradually sinking forward and downward until he finally plunged head foremost into the pit below, at the very feet of his slayer."

Finally the weight of Opdycke's counterattack proved too heavy for the Confederates. Because Hood had disposed his attacking divisions carelessly, there were no reserves to back up the initial assault and capitalize on the breakthrough. Forced to fall back, the attackers first sought refuge

inside the Federal trench line, then scrambled over the earthworks to huddle on the outer side, safe for the moment from the firestorm. Federal troops reoccupied most of the main line and threw up a barricade that plugged the gap.

It had taken the Federals less than an hour to check the assault and close the gap. But the Battle of Franklin raged on with unabated fury as Confederate attacks struck both front and flank.

The assault on the Federal left by Stewart's corps moved swiftly at first but then ran into trouble. At a railroad cut, two of Stewart's Mississippi brigades were caught in a deadly enfilading fire from Federal artillery posted across the Harpeth River to the east. Then several Confederate brigades stumbled into a grove of locust trees that the Union defenders had turned into a tough, thorny abatis. This barrier slowed the attack; Federal repeating rifles, especially those of Colonel John S. Casement's brigade, did the rest. Major General Edward C. Walthall, commanding the center division in Stewart's corps, later claimed that his troops were "under the most deadly fire of both small arms and artillery that I have ever seen troops subjected to." One of Walthall's brigades, led by Brigadier General William A. Quarles, finally broke through the abatis and rushed to the Federal earthworks, only to be pinned down there by a murderous crossfire. Quarles was wounded in the head; within hours the ranking officer in his brigade was a captain.

Artillery fire from across the river also chewed into Major General William W. Loring's division, which was advancing on the far right of the Confederate line. "The battery damaged us severely, using canister,"

wrote Captain William C. Thompson of the 6th Mississippi. "At the same time the whole division was suffering from galling musketry fire by the enemy entrenched in our immediate front."

Especially hard hit was the brigade led by Brigadier General John Adams. Seeing his men start to falter, Adams galloped forward, waving his sword and urging on his troops. Adams' headlong charge carried him directly onto the Federal earthworks. Awestruck, Lieutenant Colonel W. Scott Stewart of the 65th Illinois shouted for his men to hold their fire because, as one Federal soldier later said, "Adams was too brave to be killed." But when the Confederate general tried to snatch the 65th's flag, the color sergeant shot him down in a flash. Adams' horse was also shot and fell partly on top of him, its forelegs over the parapet. Federal soldiers

hauled the carcass off the wounded enemy general. Then they gave Adams water, but he died a few minutes later.

Still farther to the right Loring's other brigade, under Brigadier General Winfield S. Featherston, was also in trouble. Faced by withering Federal fire, the brigade advanced hesitantly, stopped, then began to fall back. This brought Loring on the scene, white with rage. A fiery individual, swift to anger, the one-armed general galloped to the head of the brigade shouting, "Great God! Do I command cowards?" Then to show the men how it was done, he turned his horse's head toward the Federal earthworks and sat motionless in the saddle for more than a minute, a perfect target in his impeccable general's uniform, sword belt about his waist, a large dark ostrich plume sweeping from his hat. Somehow, he came through unscathed.

Sword outthrust, Confederate Brigadier General John Adams gains the breastworks at Franklin astride his bay as a Union infantryman takes dead aim. Adams, a native of Nashville, had been wounded in the arm shortly before this fatal charge on November 30, 1864, and was urged to leave the field. "No," he replied, "I am going to see my men through."

114

Despite Loring's dramatic gesture, his men failed to dent the Federal line. Many of them, along with survivors from Walthall's division, were pinned down within a few yards of the Union works. Over on the Confederate left the assault also stalled. There General Bate's division had had considerable ground to cover before reaching the Federal trenches. When Bate finally got close enough to order the attack, it was almost dark. His force of Georgians and Floridians was relatively small, and the defenders — two sizable divisions commanded by Generals Nathan Kimball and Thomas Ruger — were able to hold off the Confederate charges, then pin down many of the attackers.

As dusk approached, Confederate troops along the line clung to the outer edge of the Federal works. Many hoped that if they stayed long enough the defenders would break. "We had never seen the Federals fail to run under like circumstances," boasted one Arkansas private, W. A. Washburn.

But the Federal troops were not about to abandon the fight, especially since they knew the Harpeth River was at their backs, making an orderly retreat impossible. The battle became an endurance contest, the pinned-down attackers pressing themselves to the earth, unable to go forward but perfect targets if they tried to go back. "It was fatal to leave the ditch and endeavor to escape to the rear," recalled General George Gordon, trapped there himself. "Every man who attempted it was at once exposed and shot down without exception."

In many places the two armies were separated by only a few feet. "We fought them across the breastworks," General Gordon continued, "both sides lying low and putting their guns under the head logs upon the works, firing rapidly and at random, and not exposing any part of the body except the hand that fired the gun."

Occasionally men on both sides of the barricades climbed to the top, thrust loaded pieces over and shot blindly. Some soldiers who raised their heads were seized by the hair, pulled over the parapet and killed. A number of Confederates remained in the bottom of the ditch, clutching handfuls of earth. When they saw Federal rifle barrels poking under the head log, they hurled the dirt to blind the shooters.

Across the field, the Federal musketry and artillery fire slaughtered Hood's men — officers as readily as privates. General Adams was dead. So was Brigadier General Hiram Granbury, commander of the famous Texas Brigade; he had been shot within a few yards of the Federal works. States Rights Gist, the hard-fighting South Carolinian, was also mortally wounded. Then a rumor ran through the ranks that chilled the men: Their beloved Irish-born general, Patrick Cleburne, was down.

Cleburne had ridden into action on a borrowed horse, which was killed under him. One of Cleburne's messengers, a Mississippian named James Brandon, had jumped from his own mount and handed the reins over to Cleburne. The Irishman had one leg up when a Federal cannon shot killed this second horse. At that point Cleburne, according to General Daniel Govan, had drawn his sword and started running forward on foot. "He then disappeared in the smoke of battle and that was the last time I ever saw him alive."

Sporadic firing continued as dusk deepened into night, gun flashes flickering along the trench line. Some Confederate officers concluded that their position was hopeless. General Gordon, still pinned to the earthworks, discussed the situation with a young soldier who lay beside him in the ditch. They agreed their only chance of survival was to give up. So, recalled Gordon, "we shouted to the enemy across the works to 'cease firing.' At length they understood us, and ceased their fire; we crossed the works and surrendered."

Other Confederate generals, however, were determined to continue the fight. Otho Strahl, trapped like Gordon in the ditch outside the Federal trenches, busied himself loading rifles for infantrymen to fire over the earthworks at Federals dimly visible on the other side. Not far from Strahl, Sergeant Samuel A. Cunningham of the 41st Tennessee recalled loading his Enfield and handing it to one of these brave soldiers about six times until the man "tumbled down dead into the ditch upon those killed before him." At that point Cunningham undertook the shooting. Placing himself "with one foot upon the pile of bodies and the other in the embankment," he looked down to find that General Strahl was standing among the dead, ramming charges into the Enfields and passing up the loaded guns.

Federal fire soon hit Strahl, knocking him down at Cunningham's feet. "He threw up his hands, falling on his face, and I thought him dead," Cunningham reported. But Strahl quickly "raised up, saying he was shot in the neck, and called for Colonel Stafford to turn over his command. He crawled over the dead, the ditch being three deep, about 20 feet to Colonel Stafford."

The wounded Strahl had only moments to live. "His staff officers started to carry him to the rear, but he received another shot, and directly the third, which killed him instantly."

Colonel F.E.P. Stafford, Cunningham soon discovered, had also been killed. With both of the brigade's ranking officers gone, Cunningham decided that he and the handful of men left on that part of the line were in need of new orders. Racing to the rear, he reported to division headquarters, only to find that Major General John C. Brown had also been put out of action by a serious wound. An overbearing staff officer instructed Cunningham to report to General Strahl. "This assured me," Cunningham later wrote, "that those in command did not know the real situation."

In fact, the Confederate leaders had been out of touch almost from the beginning. General Hood remained on Winstead Hill, more than two miles to the south, throughout the battle. His view was obscured by the guns' dense smoke, which hung motionless in the still air, and then by the growing darkness. The commander of Hood's largest corps, General Cheatham, was stationed at another high point, Privet Knob, his view equally obscured. The two men communicated little during the battle; neither issued any fresh orders. The commander of the other Confederate corps involved in the fight, Alexander Stewart, had his hands full on the right and could do nothing to direct the army's overall movements. Hood's third corps, headed by General Stephen Lee, was still toiling up the Columbia Pike when the battle began. Only one of Lee's divisions managed to make a belated attack, and it was repulsed. Handicapped by a lack of coordination, Hood's army had beaten itself to death in piecemeal assaults against the Fed-

In a portrait taken near war's end, Emerson Opdycke *(center)*, brevetted a brigadier general after the Battle of Franklin, sits with the regimental commanders who served in his brigade there, including Lieutenant Colonel Arthur MacArthur *(far right)* and Colonel George Washington Smith *(third from right)*. MacArthur was wounded at Franklin during Opdycke's charge; Smith's regiment seized five enemy battle flags.

eral ramparts, the soldiers fighting on their own until they were either dead, wounded or exhausted beyond caring.

On the Federal side, the hovering smoke had also obscured what was happening. But the alarm caused by the early collapse in the center of the line had been followed by a calm determination to hold on at all costs. Soon it became clear to the Union officers and men that their rifle and artillery fire were inflicting dreadful losses on the attackers. As darkness approached, Major General Jacob Cox, architect of the Federal defenses, could sense that the fight was won. "We who were upon the line knew that the impetus of Hood's assault was broken," he wrote later, "and that we could hold our position."

But General Schofield's orders to fall back across the Harpeth River and retreat to Nashville still held. Cox sent his brother and aide, Captain Theodore Cox, to Schofield's headquarters to urge a change. Hood had taken such punishment, General Cox believed, that the Federals could counterattack in the morning and destroy the enemy.

Schofield, however, would have none of it. He had been in a command post on the northern bank of the Harpeth throughout the battle and had little feel for what had taken place. And he evidently discounted the fact that while the battle was raging around Franklin, his cavalry chief, General James Wilson, had been handing the redoubtable Nathan Bedford Forrest an unprecedented shellacking. Forrest had crossed the Harpeth southeast of town with two divisions, intending to fall upon Schofield's flank and rear. Wilson, attacking in full force, had driven Forrest's troopers back upon the river and then across it. It was the first time that Forrest had been beaten by a smaller force in a stand-up fight.

Wilson's victory had removed the threat of the fast-moving Confederate cavalry. Despite this, Schofield remained uncertain, imagining that Hood's army might yet cross the river and circle in his rear. The withdrawal would proceed as ordered. The Federal troops began pulling back about 11 p.m. By midnight they were marching quietly through Franklin toward the bridges. By 3 a.m. on December 1 the men of the rear guard had crossed the river and burned the bridges behind them. The army was again on its way northward.

Schofield abandoned his wounded. Hundreds of men unable to walk were left in makeshift hospitals in Franklin to await the Confederates. Other wounded soldiers were still up on the line. So were a good number of perfectly healthy troops. To avoid alerting the enemy, Federal officers passed the order to withdraw in whispers; many men who slept in exhaustion did not hear it. They awakened the next morning to find themselves prisoners.

Before the departure, Federal Colonel Tristram T. Dow of the 112th Illinois had walked onto the field. "No enemies were there but those disabled or dead," he recalled, "and the cries of the wounded for help were very distressing."

The scene was equally appalling for the many Confederates who, despite their fatigue, were soon prowling about in the dark trying to find friends and relatives. "I could have trodden on a dead man at every step," wrote Chaplain James McNeilly, searching for his brother near the center of the Federal line. "The dead were piled up in the trenches almost to the top of the earthworks." McNeilly found his brother's corpse less than 50 yards from the Federal line, near the body of Patrick Cleburne. That gallant general, reported Private John McQuaide, the Mississippian who found him, "lay flat upon his back as if asleep." He had taken a bullet squarely in the heart. Cleburne's body was buried the next day in the beautiful churchyard at Ashwood that had brought him a moment's peace two days earlier.

Also wandering the battlefield on that dark night was an elderly slave known as Uncle Wiley Howard, a servant to General States Rights Gist. Howard found his master at last, lying in a field hospital on the Confederate far left. When the general died, Howard remained with the body until morning, then took it for burial.

All of the searchers agreed that the Franklin battlefield was a place of unmatched horror. "It was awful!" recalled Lieutenant Colonel William D. Gale, assistant adjutant general of Stewart's corps. "The ditch at the enemy's line — on the right and left of the pike — was literally filled with dead bodies lying across each other in all unseemly deformity of violent death." An Alabamian added, "I have seen many battlefields, but none to equal this."

Hood's army was now so close to disintegration that a precise count of the casualties was never made — or perhaps it was a count that no one wanted to make. Best estimates are that Hood lost a staggering 7,000 men — 1,750 killed outright, the rest wounded or taken prisoner. By contrast, Federal casualties were 1,222 killed and wounded, 1,104 missing and presumed taken prisoner. Most of the Federal casualties were from Wagner's division, incurred in the breaching of the forward line.

Confederate burial details went to work, placing a scrap of blanket over each man's face before throwing down the dirt. Stretcher parties picked up the wounded, and soon Franklin's buildings and homes were full of moaning men.

As Hood's troops grasped the magnitude of the disaster, bitterness began to grow. "Soldiers are quick to perceive blunders," wrote Captain W. O. Dodd of Forrest's cav-

A High Toll of Generals

The Battle of Franklin devastated the ranks of Confederate John Bell Hood's subordinate commanders: Six generals were killed, the worst such loss suffered by either side in a single attack during the War. Hardest hit was John Brown's division, caught in the Federal counterattack west of the turnpike to Nashville. Three of Brown's brigade commanders — Gist, Strahl and Carter — took mortal wounds there; the fourth was captured.

Of the six generals slain, only Adams is known to have died in the saddle. The others were apparently fighting on foot alongside their men when they were hit. Granbury, leader of the Texas Brigade, was found dead in the ditch below the breastworks east of the turnpike, not far from where his commander, Patrick Cleburne, stood and fell.

BRIGADIER GENERAL
JOHN CARTER

BRIGADIER GENERAL
HIRAM GRANBURY

MAJOR GENERAL
PATRICK CLEBURNE

BRIGADIER GENERAL
JOHN ADAMS

BRIGADIER GENERAL
OTHO STRAHL

BRIGADIER GENERAL
STATES RIGHTS GIST

alry. Hood had let the enemy march past him one day; on the next he had sent his own troops into "a slaughter pen to be shot down like animals." Captain Samuel T. Foster of the 24th Texas Cavalry (Dismounted) angrily recalled Hood's promise, made the month before, that he would engage in no suicidal attacks. "Gen. Hood has betrayed us," wrote Foster in his diary. "This is not the kind of fighting he promised us at Tuscumbia and Florence when we started into Tennessee. This was not a 'fight with equal numbers and choice of the ground' by no means. And the wails and cries of widows and orphans made at Franklin Tenn Nov 30th 1864 will heat up the fires of the bottomless pit to burn the soul of Gen J B Hood for Murdering their husbands and fathers at that place that day. It can't be called anything else but cold blooded Murder."

The object of this growing disgust rode slowly into Franklin later that morning of December 1. Hood stopped at the home of a Mrs. Sykes, dismounted and sat in a chair in the yard. "He looked so sad," a child remembered. Yet Hood appeared to have learned nothing from the disaster. In his memoirs written years later he still claimed that before Franklin his men had been afraid to attack breastworks — and he saw the battle not as having proved him wrong, but as having worked the cure for that ailment.

Hood was unaware how badly the struggle had crippled his army. Before learning of Schofield's nighttime retreat, he had planned to renew his attacks on the Federal earthworks at dawn. When morning revealed that the Union entrenchments were empty, Hood relentlessly ordered an immediate pursuit, sending his bone-weary, bitter and disillusioned troops up the Franklin

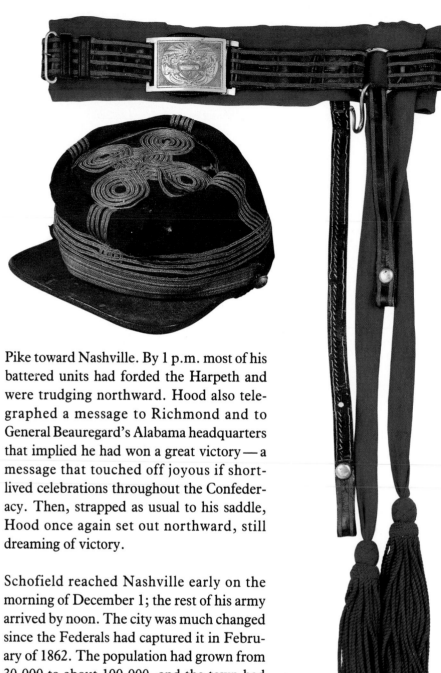

Among the articles worn in battle by Patrick Cleburne were the kepi at left, above, decorated with a general's four lines of gold braid, and the sash and sword belt fastened with a buckle bearing the coat of arms of Cleburne's home state of Arkansas. A private told of finding the general's body on the field at Franklin, "his military cap partly over his eyes."

Pike toward Nashville. By 1 p.m. most of his battered units had forded the Harpeth and were trudging northward. Hood also telegraphed a message to Richmond and to General Beauregard's Alabama headquarters that implied he had won a great victory — a message that touched off joyous if short-lived celebrations throughout the Confederacy. Then, strapped as usual to his saddle, Hood once again set out northward, still dreaming of victory.

Schofield reached Nashville early on the morning of December 1; the rest of his army arrived by noon. The city was much changed since the Federals had captured it in February of 1862. The population had grown from 30,000 to about 100,000, and the town had become a communication and distribution center to an extent unimagined in prewar days. It had also become one of the most fortified cities in America, with a series of strong points sited on commanding elevations linked by miles of entrenchments. The works were especially daunting to the south, built into a solid arc that swept from one bend in the Cumberland River east of the city to another west of town. These fortifications were backed by a reserve line in case the first should be pierced. Schofield deployed his men in the eastern segment of the main line and then reported to General Thomas.

That methodical officer had been pulling in troops from all over Tennessee as it became more and more clear that Hood's movements were aiming at Nashville. Long apprehensive that he lacked the numbers to defend the town, Thomas was now able to breathe more easily. Major General Andrew J. Smith and his 13,000-man XVI Corps had arrived on November 30 after a long, much-delayed trip from Missouri. And Schofield's arrival meant that the Federal army numbered about 50,000 and was still growing. Hood could scarcely muster 30,000, and his numbers were shrinking daily as beaten men slipped silently off toward their homes. Later Hood would assert that he had "an effective force of only 23,053."

There were other reasons for General Thomas to feel confident. His men were fresh, well fed, well armed and warmly clothed; and their supply pipeline was bulging. The Confederates on the other hand faced shortages of everything, especially the shoes, clothing and blankets needed to withstand the winter cold. In addition, Thomas felt he controlled the tactical situation. Should Hood circle Nashville and move toward the Ohio River — his old dream — he would find the massive Federal army fatally fixed on his rear. If he were to retreat toward Alabama, Thomas would follow, driving the Confederates until their army broke up.

In Thomas' view, the issue was not merely winning; it was winning so thoroughly that Hood's Army of Tennessee would be utterly destroyed. To strike such a blow, Thomas was convinced, would end the war in the west, and he was determined to do just that. Thomas smarted inwardly from a sense that

his efforts and sacrifices for the Union had never been properly appreciated in Washington — possibly because his Virginia birth still prompted some superiors to distrust his loyalty. He would prove once and for all that he was one of the Union's most valuable generals.

As often before, however, Thomas found something lacking in his military arrangements. His infantry was in fine shape and his artillery adequate, but his cavalry was distinctly not in good enough condition for the climactic campaign he had in mind. The cavalry corps was large enough — about 15,000 men — but much of it still was not mounted, and the horses that James Wilson had had in the field with Schofield were badly worn. More horses and fresh ones were needed. While waiting for Wilson to collect them, Thomas would come close to losing his command and his chance to fight Hood.

Hood arrived at the outskirts of Nashville on the evening of December 1 and by the next morning had deployed his army on a line in the Brentwood Hills, south of the city. With his lack of manpower the best he could manage was a line about four miles long, whereas the Federal lines facing him stretched more than 10 miles. Further, the Federal entrenchments covered all eight turnpikes spoking southward from the city. Hood's line barely covered four of them — the Granny White Pike and the Franklin Pike toward his center, the Nolensville Pike to the east, the Hillsboro Pike to the west. The flanks of this limited line were in the air, making them especially vulnerable to attack, and within the line Hood's men were spread dangerously thin.

Hood hoped that reinforcements would

somehow reach him and make it possible for him to attack. Lacking additional men, his plan, as he later wrote, was "to take position, entrench around Nashville, and await Thomas' attack which, if handsomely repulsed, might afford us an opportunity to follow up our advantage on the spot, and enter the city on the heels of the enemy." It was the slenderest of threads.

Schofield's attitude toward Hood changed as soon as he reached the safety of the Nashville entrenchments. Now he wanted to sally forth immediately and whip his old enemy. Before long he was deriding Thomas as an old woman for delaying. Schofield had not

hesitated to undermine superiors before.

Schofield's barbs fell on fertile ground, especially at Ulysses S. Grant's headquarters at City Point, Virginia. Grant and the Army of the Potomac had been locked in a grinding stalemate with Robert E. Lee's Army of Northern Virginia for more than five months. Grant wanted action somewhere to bolster Northern morale. So did President Lincoln, Secretary of War Edwin Stanton and Major General Henry Halleck. Why did not Thomas, with his superior force, attack immediately? What if Hood circled Nashville and made a damaging thrust to the north — or fled southward, preserving his

Battle Flags of the Defeated

The magnitude of Hood's defeat at Franklin is reflected in the number of battle flags captured by the Federals. The Union command documented the capture of 22, including those below, and claimed 11 others. The precise figure was never verified because some of

the flags, a Federal officer explained, were "torn up and sent home by the privates."

The captured colors told the history of the once-proud Army of Tennessee. The 16th Alabama's flag (below, right) had a cross-cannon insignia, granted after it overran a battery at Perryville in 1862. There as well, the 33rd Alabama earned the first battle honor on its flag (center). The combined 2nd and 6th Missouri figured in so many contests early in the War that it scarcely had room

on its banner (below, left) for further laurels.

Some of the colors taken at Franklin were captured by Federal infantrymen single-handedly. One such intrepid soldier was Sergeant Alfred Ransbottom of the 97th Ohio who, as evening fell and the Confederate attack faltered, dashed through a gap in the Federal breastworks. Battling hand-to-hand with the color-bearer of the 2nd and 6th Missouri, he grabbed the enemy flag and bore it back in triumph through the Federal lines.

CAPTURED BY THE
97TH OHIO

CAPTURED BY THE
12TH KENTUCKY

CAPTURED BY THE
104TH OHIO

army to fight another day? What, in short, if the promised victory were denied?

Thomas was hindered in the ensuing debate by his unwillingness or inability to explain fully to his superiors what to him seemed self-evident. Thomas knew that none of the dire possibilities that so alarmed Grant and Halleck at a distance would happen. He was determined to be fully prepared before he made any sort of move — and that meant getting horses.

His cavalry chief, the volatile General Wilson, who admired Thomas as much as he detested Schofield, was hard at work rounding up every thoroughbred and brewery nag he could find. He seized all of Nashville's streetcar and livery-stable horses along with the carriage and saddle horses of the gentry. Even a favorite pair owned by Andrew Johnson, the vice president-elect, were pressed into service. A circus then visiting Nashville lost every mount except its ponies; even the old white trick horse was confiscated.

But all of Wilson's preparations took time, and Grant was impatient from the start. "You should attack before he fortifies," Grant wired Thomas on December 2, adding a couple of hours later, "You will now suffer incalculable injury upon your railroads if Hood is not speedily disposed of. Put forth, therefore, every possible exertion to attain this end. Should you get him to retreating, give him no peace."

Nettled, Thomas answered that he had the situation well in hand and would attack as soon as his cavalry force was large enough to contend with Forrest. But Stanton and Lincoln kept prodding and so did Grant, who on December 7 fired a heavy gun: "Attack Hood at once and await no longer the remount of your cavalry."

About this time, realizing that someone was feeding Washington damaging reports, Thomas' staff officers nosed about and discovered the draft of a critical wire in Schofield's handwriting. "Why does he send such telegrams?" Thomas said wonderingly to one of his division commanders, Major General James B. Steedman. Steedman recalled afterward that he had "smiled at the noble old soldier's simplicity and said, 'General Thomas, who is next in command to you and would succeed you in case of removal?' 'Oh, I see,' he said as he mournfully shook his head." And in fact, Grant was considering replacing Thomas with Schofield.

Feeling the pressure acutely, Thomas hurried his preparation and on December 8 issued orders setting the attack for December 10. But then the weather caused a further delay. On December 9 the worst storm of the winter struck, with torrents of sleet that sheeted central Tennessee in glittering ice. The temperature plummeted and the ground froze solid. Thomas postponed the attack.

In the Confederate lines the misery was intense. "We are suffering more for shoes than anything else, and there is no chance to get new ones," wrote Captain Sam Foster in his diary. "At Brigade Head Quarters there has been established a Shoe Shop, not to make shoes, for there is no leather, but they take an old worn out pair of shoes and sew Moccasins over them of green cow hide with the hair side in. The shoe is put on and kept there, and as the hide dries it draws closer and closer to the old shoe."

The Confederate troops were suffering as well from lack of shelter. The men had to retreat to holes they hacked in the frozen earth. A few feet deep and lined with twigs, these offered a little warmth to three men

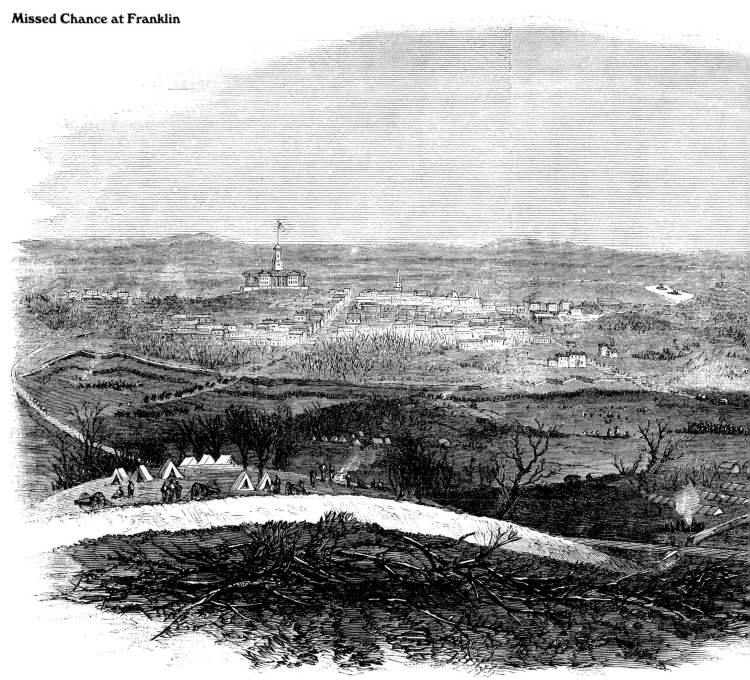

under a couple of blankets. The holes were, however, uncomfortably like graves, one Confederate noted.

It was no time to move an army. Sergeant Major William R. Hartpence of the 51st Indiana observed that "everything was covered with ice an inch thick, as far as the eye could reach, and walking was still extremely difficult and dangerous." But a storm in Tennessee made little impression on Washington, and the telegrams bombarding Thomas now included threats. Harassed and hurt, he answered quietly: "I feel con-

scious I have done everything in my power to prepare, and that the troops could not have been gotten ready before this. If General Grant should order me to be relieved, I will submit without a murmur."

The dignity of this message reflects the calm imperturbability that many of Thomas' officers and men most admired in their commander. "He was by no means a rapid thinker or a brilliant conversationalist, but his mind was well stored with all sorts of military information," wrote James Wilson. "His self control was perfect, his bearing

A sketch of Nashville's defenses viewed from the south reveals the Federals' heavily fortified outer line, bordered by tent camps; a second line skirts the city in the middle distance. The state capitol (*background, left*) drew the attention of Hood's Confederates as they approached from Franklin: One Tennessean recalled that he could "see the Stars and Stripes flying from the dome."

lofty and serene, and in all that he said and did he reminded me of the traditional Washington more than any man I had ever met. He was a patriot without flaw and a soldier without reproach."

The authorities in Washington, however, saw Thomas only as the "Rock of Chickamauga," an unshakable fighter on defense but lacking the aggressiveness required for the offense. Even Grant succumbed to this view and, his patience running out, ordered Thomas' relief — not by Schofield but by Major General John A. Logan, a bold fighter who had served with Grant in the Vicksburg Campaign of 1863. Logan was to leave Washington for Nashville immediately and take over if Thomas had not already attacked. The next day, fuming, Grant left Petersburg and started for Nashville himself. He went via Washington and was there when word finally came: The attack had started.

Hood meanwhile had been making preparations for the enemy assault he hoped to convert to his own triumph. The price of his frontal attack at Franklin was felt everywhere; units were shrunk in size, some were combined with others and most were commanded by junior officers. Undaunted, however, by either his army's weakness or its sufferings, he ordered frequent roll calls to discourage deserters and had his engineers lay out cunning entrenchments that took advantage of the rough, broken terrain. The men cleared swaths through wooded areas to open up fields of fire, then shaped the felled trees into abatis. Artillerymen positioned guns in pits along the line, set to rake attackers with canister.

What troops remained of Cheatham's battered corps were on the Confederate far right, across the Nolensville Pike; the east-

ern end of their line swung forward along a railroad cut that would make it difficult for enemy attackers to approach. The center of the Confederate line was held by Stephen Lee's corps. These men were relatively fresh, having in the main missed Franklin. Lee's position reached from the Franklin Pike to the Granny White Pike, the latter named for a long-dead widow whose tavern had been a local institution.

Stewart's corps, badly hurt at Franklin, held the Confederate left, reaching to the Hillsboro Pike. There Stewart's line bent back, the men digging rifle pits and working on a series of five redoubts. The redoubts — only three were actually completed — were designed to be impregnable little forts with as many as 50 artillerists working four guns in each one and with 100 infantrymen in support. The redoubts were supposed to protect Hood's vulnerable left flank, which the massive Federal line overlapped by several miles.

Then, with all his hopes pinned on withstanding an assault so well that a counterattack might succeed, Hood made an inexplicable move. On December 7 he sent most of Forrest's horsemen as well as some infantry units to attack the town of Murfreesboro, 30 miles to the southeast, holding back only one division of cavalry under Brigadier General James R. Chalmers. Perhaps Hood thought that Thomas would respond by detaching troops to reinforce Major General Lovell Rousseau's Murfreesboro garrison and thus weaken his own force at Nashville. If that was Hood's scheme, it did not succeed. Forrest's raid accomplished little, and the cavalry's absence cost Hood many of his best fighters, reducing sharply his already-slender chances in the battle to come. Only

125

when the Federal attack was imminent did Hood attempt to recall Forrest — who failed to get back in time.

Thomas scheduled his attack to begin as soon as a thaw showed signs of melting Nashville's carapace of ice. On December 14 he called his officers to his room in the city's St. Cloud Hotel and gave them written orders for a massive, coordinated assault modeled on classic lines. It would begin with a feint on the Federal left, to hold the Confederate right in place. The diversion would be made by James Steedman's division, which included the 1st and 2nd Colored Brigades.

The main attack would come on the Federal right and it would strike the most vulnerable spot in the Confederate line, the exposed left flank defended by Stewart's battered corps. This main thrust would be delivered by Andrew J. Smith's Missouri divisions; by IV Corps under Brigadier General Thomas J. Wood, who had replaced the wounded Stanley; and by a division of cavalry led by Brigadier General Edward Hatch. Schofield's XXIII Corps would be in reserve, positioned to reinforce the main attack. Wilson's cavalry would be on the far right to screen the Federal flank and attempt to envelop the Confederates.

During the night, heavy fog formed and at 4 a.m. on the 15th, when bugles sounded, the men found themselves groping for position. Thomas checked out of the St. Cloud with luggage packed and mounted his horse under gaslights that shone dimly. He was wearing a new uniform, gold braid faintly gleaming. The air felt warm; when the fog burned off, the day would be sunny.

On the left, Steedman's three brigades, about 7,600 men with two batteries, moved forward into a blinding white mist. "Before six o'clock the brigade was in motion," recalled Captain Henry V. Freeman of the 12th U.S. Colored Troops. "Everyone knew it could not go far in that direction without someone getting hurt." The 12th was made up mainly of former slaves. They had not been in combat before; this was their chance to prove themselves. There had been some question of whether men of such background would make good soldiers, but their officers, all white volunteers, had great confidence in them.

Steedman ordered Freeman and his men to charge just as the fog began to lift. The black troops rushed up a long hill and overran the railroad cut that was supposed to help anchor the far right of Cheatham's line. Then Freeman led his regiment over a ridge — and into heavy fire. The men nevertheless plunged forward, quickly taking the advance rifle pits and threatening the main Confederate works. There the attack bogged down, but for hours the untried troops made things hot for the defenders. Their "staying qualities," said Freeman, "were here well tested." Steedman staged a second attack about 11 a.m. and kept pressure on the Confederate right all day.

As designed, this pressure fixed Cheatham in place. It also helped hold Stephen Lee's entire corps in the center. Lee's men were threatened on both right and left as the battle developed, but if they moved in either direction the Federals could move straight down the Franklin Pike and split Hood's army in two. Lee did manage to send four brigades to aid Stewart, but the rest of his corps remained in position throughout the fighting, immobilized by Thomas' well-conceived tactics. That left Stewart's men virtually on

Major General George Thomas, shown here with the pocket compass he carried throughout the War, was a stickler for detail, once stating that "the fate of an army may depend on a buckle." But his troops admired him for his methodical ways. Thomas spared no pains, an aide said, to see that his army was "well supplied, well looked after, and always brought to the right place at the right time."

their own against the main Union attack.

The movement on the Federal right was delayed by the fog, which finally cleared about 9 a.m. Then the soldiers, looking back toward Nashville, saw that they were under the gaze of a large crowd of spectators, most of them evidently Nashville natives and Confederate sympathizers. "All the hills in our rear were black with human beings watching the battle, but silent," recalled Colonel Isaac R. Sherwood. "No army on the continent ever played on any field to so large and so sullen an audience."

As these critical observers watched, the Federal attack on the right suffered embarrassing delays. Mud made progress slow; in some spots the infantry was hardly able to waddle forward through the slippery mire. Then the flamboyant Wilson, his horsemen eager to brush back the Confederate cavalry screen and extend the envelopment of Stewart's flank, found his troopers stymied by Brigadier General John McArthur's division of Smith's corps, which inadvertently had crossed in front of Wilson's line of advance. The delays enabled Hood to shore up his left with the few reserves he possessed — a handful of cavalry and Brigadier General Matthew D. Ector's infantry brigade, its six regiments depleted to a mere 700 men.

At last the Federal advance gained momentum. Wilson, moving forward with about 12,000 men, began to meet and push back Chalmers' single division of Confederate cavalry. At the same time Andrew J. Smith, entrusted with delivering the main blow, lurched forward with a like number of infantry and, fording several creeks, approached Stewart's strung-out line. The men of Ector's understrength brigade fired a few rounds but then hastily fell back, as instruct-

ed, over a ridge, making a run for the main line and those protective redoubts along the Hillsboro Pike.

While Wilson's cavalry and Smith's infantry advanced on the Federal far right, the men of Wood's IV Corps were moving forward slowly in the Federal center. They too had started in fog, wrote Sergeant Major Hartpence, and when the sun broke through, the men of the 51st Indiana saw on each side "the double line of soldiers gradually dwindling, till they seemed like a thread of blue yarn, with here and there a patch of red where the colors appeared."

Soon Wood's corps was moving up the

Federal quartermasters and rear-echelon troops gather on a barren hillside in Nashville on December 15 to watch the battle for that city unfold. The ghostly figure standing at left shifted his position while the photograph was being taken, causing his image to be superimposed on that of the spectators beyond.

northwestern slope of Montgomery Hill, the most advanced part of the Confederate line. Hood had already withdrawn the bulk of his troops from the hill, but a number remained, including some sharpshooters hidden in a fine brick house that topped the rise. The marksmen peppered the advancing Federals until an Ohio battery put a shell right through a window. "Then came the signal to advance," Sergeant Major Hartpence recalled, "and we started off on a quick-step that soon increased to a run." Bullets whistled as the men passed through an abatis. "Then came the command to 'charge with a yell!' And such a yell as we gave!

"On and up we rushed," Hartpence continued, "every fellow trying to gain the rebel works first — shooting, loading, yelling." Then Hartpence saw one of the officers of the 51st Indiana gallop up to the regimental color-bearer, Sergeant John Young, and snatch the staff, the quicker to plant the flag on the Confederate works. "The officer put spurs to his horse, leaving the regiment behind, but taking with him the plucky color-sergeant, who did not propose to relinquish the colors, but was determined to plant them there himself." The struggle at the Confederate earthworks was so violent that the officer was pulled from his horse, whereupon Sergeant Young again grabbed the staff and drove it "into the soft dirt on the top of the rebel works." The 51st Indiana, Hartpence concluded in triumph, "had taken Montgomery Hill while the johnnies fled in dire confusion." The Federal line swept over the Confederate trenches, taking both prisoners and guns.

But this was only an advanced Confederate line; the bulk of the troops had withdrawn to another line beyond. Immediately, however, said Corporal George W. Herr of the 59th Illinois, there "followed one of those remarkable occurrences where the rank and file outgeneraled their general. On reaching the enemy's works, the men in the advance could plainly see another line of entrenchments farther on and to which the routed enemy were fleeing." Nearly every officer on the line gave the command to halt, Herr continued, "but all to no purpose; the men were, using their own language, 'bound to have the next line,' which they did."

On their own, the men of Herr's brigade hurtled forward, riding their own momentum. "They soon came to the edge of an open field from which point, and about 300 yards directly in front, could be seen a strong line of earthworks, alive with men and bristling with bayonets, interspersed with batteries of artillery." But the sight did not daunt the attackers, Herr recalled. The men in the line seemed to cry "Forward!" simultaneously, then rushed through the abatis "and over the works, capturing many prisoners, two flags and four pieces of artillery."

This extraordinary charge broke the center of Stewart's line, sending Confederates running for the rear. The retreat was quickened when Stewart's men saw another Union column emerging on their flank — Smith's men striking from the other side. Against a frontal assault alone, Stewart's thin-stretched line might have been able to rally and hold. But the knowledge that the defense on the far left was swiftly breaking up was too much. With the flank gone, the entire line would inevitably collapse.

On the Confederate left, only the redoubts on Hillsboro Pike stood in the path of the Federal onslaught. From Redoubt No. 1, the strongest of the forts, the Confederate line turned back at a right angle and ran along the pike to Redoubts Nos. 2 and 3. Farther down the pike, well to the rear of the main line, were the incompleted redoubts, Nos. 4 and 5.

It was obvious to Stewart that both Andrew J. Smith's XVI Corps and Hatch's cavalry were going to strike the redoubts with overwhelming force. In desperation, Stewart turned to General Edward Walthall's division, which had been held in reserve. Walthall posted the bulk of his troops behind the stone wall that ran much of the distance between Redoubts Nos. 3 and 4, also sending two batteries of guns, each pro-

tected by a company of infantry, to defend the two unfinished redoubts. As the survivors of Ector's tattered little brigade came in, retreating before the Federal juggernaut, Walthall put them at the extreme end of the line defending the stone wall. But this still left them well short of the last redoubt, which stood like a tiny island soon to be lapped by a sea of blue. His entire defensive line, recalled Stewart, "was stretched to the utmost tension."

The first stronghold to fall was the unsupported fifth redoubt. Stewart and his men watched helplessly as Hatch's cavalry surged over a ridge, enveloped the fort, then dismounted for the attack. No one told the horsemen to remove their cavalry sabers, and so the troopers were encumbered by the dragging scabbards as they charged in company with a couple of Federal brigades up the hill and toward the parapet. Lieutenant Colonel John H. Stibbs of the 12th Iowa, watching from a nearby ridge, first saw enemy gun flashes darting toward the attackers and the Federals disappearing into the smoke. But then, Stibbs recalled, "we heard a mighty cheer and a moment later we saw the flashes of the guns in the opposite direction" as Hatch's troopers turned the captured cannon on the fleeing Confederates.

Next to come under attack was Redoubt No. 4. In command there was Captain Charles L. Lumsden, a graduate of the Virginia Military Institute and an experienced artilleryman. Lumsden had 100 infantrymen posted in shallow ditches on each side of the redoubt and four guns within the ramparts. His orders were to hold on "as long as you can." He was determined to do so. Under fire from the captured cannon in Redoubt No. 5, he shifted two of his smoothbore

Early on December 15, General George Thomas launched an assault on John Bell Hood's Confederate army south of Nashville. James Steedman's division moved first on the Federal left, attacking Benjamin Cheatham's line at dawn to divert attention from the main thrust to the west. There, at midday, the bulk of Thomas' army attacked Alexander Stewart's strung-out Confederates. The Federal IV Corps under Thomas Wood took Montgomery Hill while elements of John Schofield's XXIII Corps and James Wilson's cavalry enveloped Hood's left flank, sending the Confederates reeling. By evening Hood had patched together a new line of defense from Shy's Hill to Overton Hill, in readiness for a renewed Federal assault the next morning.

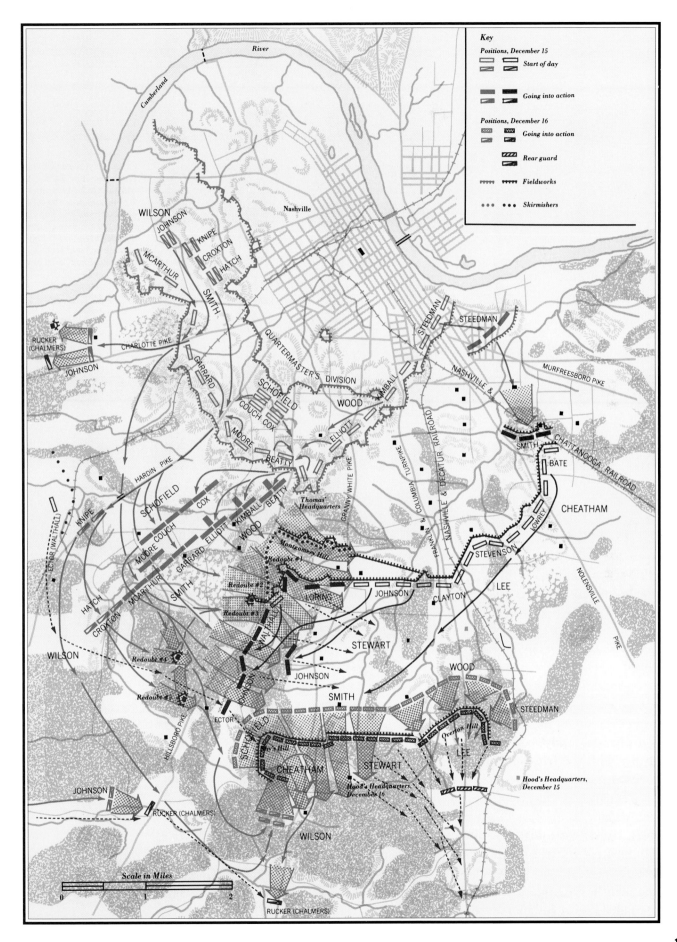

Colonel Sylvester Hill lurches back in his saddle at near left after being shot while his brigade storms a Confederate redoubt near the Hillsboro Pike on December 15. The Federals overwhelmed the defenders so swiftly that they suffered few casualties; Hill and a single enlisted man in his brigade were killed and 36 were wounded.

Napoleons to answer, firing the other two at Smith's corps coming in from the west. It was soon evident that his position was hopeless, but Lumsden fought on, his guns booming, infantry muskets crackling alongside. One of the defenders, Sergeant James R. Maxwell, recalled helping work the guns until only a handful of men were left. At that point, he looked up to see Lumsden himself standing in the redoubt with a charge of canister in his hands, ready to keep on firing. The gunner with the friction primers had fled, however, making it impossible to discharge the Napoleons. Only then did Lumsden admit defeat, calling out: "Take care of yourselves, boys." With that the survivors, Maxwell included, turned tail and "lit out down the hill."

As the men in his brigade watched two redoubts fall, Colonel Stibbs remembered,

they went wild, shouting that they wanted to assault one of the strong points themselves. "Bring us a fort! Bring us a fort!" they yelled as General Smith rode by. The general wheeled his horse. "Never mind, I'll get a fort for you and you won't have to wait long for it either!"

Stibbs's men swiftly threw their blankets, canteens, haversacks and other heavy equipment on the ground, readying themselves for a headlong charge. "Waist belts were tightened a notch, bayonets fixed, the priming in every musket examined," Stibbs later wrote, and a look of grim determination came over his men's faces.

Their objective was to be Redoubt No. 3. General Smith remarked that it looked tough from where he stood, but Stibbs's brigade commander, Colonel Sylvester Hill, said, "Oh, no, our men will go right up there;

An Iowan who saw action in the Red River Campaign before being posted to Tennessee, Colonel Hill was conditioned to the vicissitudes of war. At Louisiana's Yellow Bayou in May 1864 he was wounded while leading a charge. In the same battle his son, Fred, serving as an orderly, fell as his father would at Nashville — killed by a bullet to the head.

nothing can stop them." Smith told them to wait until he could coordinate a supporting attack, but within a minute, Hill ordered his bugler to sound the charge and the men were on the way. Soon Hill was dead with a bullet through his head. The Federals swept up a rise to the redoubt while the Confederates, unable to depress their guns low enough to rake the enemy, limbered up and raced for Redoubt No. 2.

Once there, the Confederate artillerists "sent a storm of grape and canister into our ranks," said a soldier in the 7th Minnesota. "There did not seem," added one of the regiment's officers, Captain Theodore Carter, "to be ten second intervals between the discharges." But neither the Minnesotans nor the men of Stibbs's 12th Iowa paused for more than a few moments before charging once again and capturing Redoubt No. 2. The troops poured over the earthworks, Captain Carter recalled, "the Confederates leaving the fort as we got to it."

By 1:30 in the afternoon Stewart's position along the Hillsboro Pike had become untenable. Wilson's cavalrymen were ranging unobstructed far in the rear. Schofield's corps had joined Wood's and Smith's in pounding the Confederate defenses. Walthall's division had been driven back from the stone wall and was breaking up. Four redoubts were gone and now the most important of them all, No. 1, the anchor point that held Stewart's line, was under savage fire from two sides. Stewart began pulling back, hoping to take a new position on the Granny White Pike. Last to withdraw were parts of a Mississippi brigade commanded by Brigadier General Claudius Sears. Extricating the last of his men as two Federal brigades surged over the works, Sears paused for a final look at the lost redoubt. Just then a solid shot severed his leg.

Despite the intense Federal pressure, the Confederate withdrawal did not degenerate into a rout. A few units panicked, but most of the men retreated in order. As Stewart's men fell back toward the Granny White Pike, Lee's troops in the center also moved to the rear. Soon Cheatham started a shift that took his corps all the way from the right end of the Confederate line to the far left.

December darkness was falling swiftly as the men of Hood's army, fighting to delay the Federals' pursuit, improvised a new line more than two miles south of their original positions. The Federals slowed their advance and then halted, some units going into bivouac. A number of Union officers regretted that Thomas did not continue the chase. There was a chance, they thought, to crush the Confederates even in the dark. But the rank and file were generally glad for a rest. More than nine hours had passed since the first attacks of the morning. "I thought we had done well enough for that day," summed up one soldier of the 7th Minnesota.

Although the Confederate troops did not flee, they seemed to some observers to have lost all taste for fighting. Lieutenant Colonel William D. Gale, one of Stewart's staff officers, watched as streams of soldiers moved past him to the rear. To Gale, "The men seemed utterly lethargic and without interest in battle. I never witnessed such want of enthusiasm and began to fear for tomorrow, hoping General Hood would retreat during the night." But Hood was still undaunted. He would fight again.

"The Place for Brave Men to Die"

"I was unwilling to abandon the ground as long as I saw a shadow of probability of victory; the troops would, I believed, return better satisfied even after defeat if, in grasping at the last straw, they felt that a brave and vigorous effort had been made to save the country from disaster."

MAJOR GENERAL JOHN B. HOOD AFTER THE BATTLE OF NASHVILLE

5

In the darkness Hood moved about purposefully, preparing his men for a counterattack in the morning. He still anticipated having a chance to hurl back Thomas' legions, force them to flee and then follow them into Nashville. He organized his new line about two miles back from his original position; it had necessarily tightened, forming a more compact defense than that of the previous day.

The new line was less than two miles long. It covered only two of the eight turnpikes — the Granny White on the left and the Franklin on the right — and was anchored at either end by commanding hills. On the left, just west of the Granny White Pike, was the hill that would be known after this day as Shy's Hill, for the man who would defend it to his death. On the right, just east of the Franklin Pike, was Overton Hill, which many men called Peach Orchard Hill for its spindly trees. Hood shifted Stewart's badly battered corps to the center; he moved Cheatham's relatively fresh corps to the far left to cover Shy's Hill. Cheatham's own left bent back in a great arc around the hill to protect the Confederate army's vulnerable left flank. General Stephen Lee's corps shifted to the right and fixed on Overton Hill. Hood posted his single cavalry division under General Chalmers at the end of Cheatham's line. Forrest meanwhile was hurrying back from Murfreesboro with the bulk of the cavalry, but he would not arrive until the battle was over.

It was an exhausting night for the Confederates. Officers and sergeants stood in roadways calling out their unit designations and gathering their men from the stragglers. When the regiments were reassembled and in their new positions, the men started entrenching. Soldiers who had fought all day now worked all night, and Hood's troops were approaching the limits of endurance.

That night, Thomas sent a wire to Halleck in Washington and another to his wife in New York reporting the day's success. The commission in General Logan's pocket to take over the army would not be needed. Grant fired off a return wire with perfunctory congratulations and long admonitions not to let Hood escape; telegrams from Lincoln and Stanton echoed Grant's message.

Morning found the bulk of the Union troops some distance from the new Confederate front, since most of the units had bivouacked where darkness caught them. They moved up slowly toward Hood's line over ground churned into gumbo; except for a few cavalry skirmishes, no fighting occurred throughout the long morning.

The Federals were deployed in the order of the day before. James Steedman was placed on the far left, his line curving southward around Overton Hill. To his right was Wood. Andrew J. Smith held a long stretch in the center; Schofield's corps had moved to the right of Smith's corps and was bent around Shy's Hill. Wilson's cavalry was to Schofield's right. Thomas' plan remained

unchanged: to pin down the Confederate right with a demonstration in force and then overwhelm Hood's left.

In the morning, Federal artillery fixed precisely on the new Confederate positions and opened a devastating fire. "It was uncommonly fine," recalled Wood. "It was really entertaining to watch it." A Confederate officer described the bombardment as unsurpassed "for heaviness, continuance and accuracy." Confederate gunners tried to answer, but their pieces were few and their powder poor. Among Stephen Lee's guns was the 3rd Maryland Battery, which moved forward and began improving its position on a rise, the men dragging rails from a fence 200 yards to the front to erect a crude breastwork. The battery commander, Lieutenant William L. Ritter, writing of himself in the third person, remembered, "The enemy, discovering the working party, opened on them with six guns. As they fired by battery, the men were able to continue their work in the intervals of firing, lying down when the Lieutenant, guided by the smoke from the enemy's guns, directed them."

The bombardment presaged a powerful Federal assault on Overton Hill. Colonel Philip Sidney Post, the feisty brigade commander who had spearheaded the attack that captured Montgomery Hill the day before, believed his men could carry Overton Hill by charging the west side. Wood ordered him to try, with the support of Colonel Abel D. Streight's brigade. Simultaneously, Colonel Charles R. Thompson's 2nd Colored Brigade was to storm the hill from the east. "At 3 p.m.," wrote Corporal George W. Herr of the 59th Illinois, "the men stripped themselves of all encumbrances and with the 59th in advance," they followed Colonel Post into battle.

In Streight's brigade, Sergeant Major William Hartpence of the 51st Indiana remembered the action as he and his comrades struggled up the steep slope: "The Rebels on the summit got such range of us that they slashed the canister and solid shot into us with a prodigality that was appalling. We were compelled to lie down."

The Federal batteries opened up, signaling a renewal of the attack. Streight's brigade stood up and charged with Thompson's black soldiers at its side. Then, recalled Sergeant Major Hartpence, "the enemy rose and poured into us a fire of grape, canister, shrapnel and musketry so terrific and destructive that we were compelled to fall back with great loss."

Terrain divided the 12th and 13th U.S. Colored Troops as they charged. Captain Freeman of the 12th remembered: "The brigade had not advanced fifty feet before it was smitten by the storm. A shell took a file of men from one company, burying itself in the ground at the feet of the company following. Men were falling on all sides."

135

On the far side of a cornfield, as they approached the Confederate main line, the Federals encountered a barrier of sharpened stakes and an abatis beyond it. The abatis, Freeman wrote, "caught and held the weary men like flies in a spider's web." Despite all the obstacles, some troops of the 13th Colored Infantry managed to reach the Confederate breastworks and mount the rampart. As they did so, however, Colonel Post, in plain view of his troops, was felled by a bullet and severely wounded. His loss broke the impetus of the Federal charge. At this trying moment, Corporal Herr said, the Confederates "poured in a fire which no troops could endure. For a moment the brigade halted, then came the order to fall back!"

Hartpence remembered the confusion of the Federal retreat. "How we got away at all, alive, no one will ever tell. Showers of lead — whole sheets of blue liquid lead — seemed to pour over those Rebel earthworks. But we got back. O, yes; we had to. Some of us ran backward most of the way because we didn't like the idea of being found with a hole in our back."

The Federals retreated down the slopes to the foot of Overton Hill. But the failed attack had not been in vain: Its fury had so alarmed Hood that he had pulled Patrick Cleburne's division — now led by Brigadier General James A. Smith — from a crucial po-

Deployed in columns at Overton Hill with the 59th Illinois leading, the five regiments of Colonel Philip Sidney Post's brigade follow their commander, shown galloping with sword brandished, up the slope toward Lee's guns. The men advanced "in perfect silence," an aide to General Thomas wrote, "with orders to halt for nothing, but to gain the works at a run."

sition on Shy's Hill and sent it off to the right to support Stephen Lee, who needed no help. Lee sent Cleburne's men back, but by then it was too late.

Hood's problems on his left had begun that morning when the aggressive Federal cavalryman, Wilson, began to apply pressure with his dismounted troopers, who were armed with Spencer repeating carbines. By early afternoon, the troopers had advanced across the Granny White Pike and were threatening the Franklin Pike, the last Confederate line of retreat. Now Hood was paying the price for having detached Forrest and most of the cavalry before the battle. General Chalmers and his remnants of Confederate troopers were trying to hold off Wilson's men, but the Federals pressed in on a long, slanting line, squeezing harder and harder against the rear of Shy's Hill.

The Confederates deployed on that hill were, moreover, in a vulnerable position. The defense of the hill had originally been assigned to Ector's brigade, but during the morning Hood had ordered Ector's exhausted men off the hill to confront Wilson's dismounted cavalry to the south. At that time General William Bate's division of Cheatham's corps was ordered to hold Shy's Hill. When Cleburne's division made its unnecessary shift to the right, Bate's line was stretched leftward and the defense of the hill fell to Brigadier General Thomas B. Smith's brigade. With Smith was the 37th Tennessee, commanded by a 25-year-old colonel named William M. Shy. Earlier, as Bate climbed the hill that would take the young Shy's name, he was appalled at the state of its defenses. Ector's men, working in the dark and nearing exhaustion, had built their breastworks in the wrong place — and the

constant and ferocious Federal barrage made it impossible to change them. The breastworks were so far from the crest of this very steep hill that the Confederates could not cover most of the slope; the approaching enemy would be sheltered from their fire. To make matters worse, the Confederates had not built an abatis or other barrier: When attackers came over the crest of the hill, no more than 20 yards from the breastworks, there would be no obstacles to slow them down. The situation was hazardous for the defenders — but the Federals remained ignorant of the enemy's vulnerability for most of the day, so formidable did the hills loom.

A dull, cold rain had started at noon. The Federal troops were in position and Wilson was closing his vise, but the main attack against Shy's Hill on the Federal right did not begin. The afternoon wore on, and behind the Confederate lines Hood was thinking of a counterattack for the next day.

Finally Wilson grew angry. His gains to the south of Shy's Hill might come to nothing if the Federals elsewhere failed to attack. His ire was substantially directed toward Schofield, who commanded the infantry that faced the hill. "I sent my staff officers, one after another, to Generals Schofield and Thomas with information of our success, accompanied by suggestions that the infantry should attack with vigor."

A junior general — even a hell-for-leather cavalry officer like Wilson — could say only so much. When he captured a message from Hood imploring the Confederate cavalry to "drive the Yankee cavalry from our rear or all is lost," Wilson sent three officers to Schofield, urging him to attack. When nothing happened, Wilson himself galloped off to find Thomas.

As it turned out, Schofield was responsible for the delay. He thought Shy's Hill was too formidable to attack without more men, and he wanted another division. Thomas, his patience worn thin, rode over to Schofield's position for a meeting. Wilson thus found them together, on the lee side of a small hill. As he approached, he could see in the distance his own cavalrymen behind the enemy position.

"For God's sake," he cried, "order an attack! My men are in Hood's rear. You can see their guidons fluttering behind that hill."

Thomas raised his glasses to study the hill. At last he said, in response to Schofield's protests, "The battle must be fought, even if men *are* killed."

Meanwhile, General John McArthur, a division commander in Smith's XVI Corps, was chafing. He held the position to Schofield's left, facing Shy's Hill from the north. McArthur already had asked permission to attack, but Thomas wanted the Federal assault to be coordinated. Now, with scarcely an hour of daylight left, McArthur took strong action. Convinced he could take Shy's

Hill, he sent a firm message to Smith: He would attack unless Smith said no. When he did not receive a negative response, McArthur readied his division. "With orders to the men to fix bayonets, not to fire a shot and neither to halt nor to cheer until they had gained the enemy's works, the charge was sounded," Captain Henry Stone wrote later. They "moved swiftly down the slope, across the narrow valley and began scrambling up the steep hillside."

Thomas, still conferring with Schofield and Wilson, watched the attack through his field glasses. He lowered them, glanced at Schofield and said "General Smith is attacking without waiting for you. Please advance your entire line." Faced with a direct order, Schofield sent his units forward so rapidly that much of the action was over before Wilson, galloping madly, could get back to his troopers. Cold rain in their faces, lowering clouds darkening with oncoming night, Schofield's troops started up that steep hill. Soon they were winded, but then they realized with grateful surprise that the hill itself sheltered them from enemy fire. Meanwhile,

Officers of the 111th Ohio, commanded by Lieutenant Colonel Isaac Sherwood *(standing, far right),* assemble with their shredded U.S. flag in December 1864 before the Battle of Nashville. Many in the regiment still bore the marks of earlier battles when they were called on to support the attack at Shy's Hill on the 16th. Captain Patrick Dowling *(seated, arm in sling)* had been wounded at Franklin as he plugged a break in the line and helped drive the foe back.

138

McArthur's men went crashing forward.

Colonel John H. Stibbs of the 12th Iowa, in McArthur's 3rd Brigade, watched as the 1st Brigade led the attack, running forward silently. Then the 2nd started; it fell under heavy Confederate fire immediately, but, Stibbs recalled, "there was no wavering or halting." Then the 3rd "took up the charge," he said. As he came through a cornfield he saw that the Confederates had deployed an extensive skirmish line to their front. Off to the right, Schofield's troops were going up Shy's Hill from the west. Then Stibbs noticed the Confederate skirmishers ahead of him were watching Schofield's attack on the hill instead of guarding their own front.

"They did not discover us until we were fairly on them, when they rose in a body and started for cover. With a wild shout my men started in pursuit, the most rapid runners went to the front, and in an instant our line had lost its formation, and we seemed to have become a howling mob. My men were amongst them capturing them right and left. In less time than it takes to tell it, we had captured guns, caissons, colors and prisoners galore."

Smith's men broke the Confederate line just east of Shy's Hill and poured through the gap. General Thomas, watching through his glasses, grew confused at the sight of Federal soldiers behind the Confederate line. Thomas cried to Smith, "What is the matter, are your men being captured there?"

Smith whirled on his commander. "Not by a damn sight! My men are capturing them, those are Rebel prisoners you see." Later Smith said it was the only time he had ever known General Thomas to laugh aloud.

On Shy's Hill, the Confederates were desperate. They were taking fire from front, left and rear. The brigade posted against the Federal cavalry, its senior officers shot down, collapsed when Wilson's men appeared at its rear. But the Tennesseans and Georgians on the hill held. Colonel Shy bunched the men of the 37th Tennessee in a tight formation; they were ready with the bayonet as the Federal troops came over the crest of the hill and made for the breastworks. With men falling all around him, Shy reached down to pick up a musket from a fallen soldier. As he did so he took a bullet in the head and was killed. Shortly afterward, the doomed defense broke; not more than 65 men on the hill escaped death or capture. The memorable but hopeless struggle had not staved off disaster, for now Hood's line was melting away.

Watching from the Union lines, Captain Stone reported it this way: "Beset on both sides, Bate's people broke out of the works and ran down the hill toward their right and rear. It was more like a scene in a spectacular drama than a real incident in war. The hillside in front, still green, dotted with the boys in blue swarming up the slope; the dark background of high hills beyond; the lowering clouds; the waving flags; the smoke slowly rising through the leafless tree-tops and drifting across the valleys; the wonderful outburst of musketry; the ecstatic cheers; the multitude racing for life down into the valley below.

"In those few minutes," Stone added, "an army was changed into a mob." Confederate Colonel William D. Gale saw it all happen from his position just behind Cheatham's lines. "Bate gave way and they poured over in clouds behind Walthall, which of course forced him to give way and then by brigades

Brigadier General John McArthur, the division commander who launched the Federal assault on Shy's Hill, did battle in the headdress of his native Scotland, a bonnet made official by a U.S. emblem. He came to America around 1850 and mastered the rudiments of tactics before the War as captain of a militia company, the Chicago Highland Guards.

Confederate Lieutenant Colonel William Shy, who was killed while leading a brigade at Nashville on the 16th of December, was eulogized by superiors for his "gallant and obstinate" defense of the hill that would thenceforth bear his name. His body, found on the crest, was buried at the Shy family estate near Franklin.

Minnesotans of McArthur's division forge ahead to pierce the Confederate defenses on Shy's Hill on __

December 16. They met fierce resistance, corps commander Andrew J. Smith wrote, "but nothing save annihilation could stop the onward progress of that line."

the whole line from left to right. All control over them was gone and they flatly refused to stop, throwing down their guns, every man for himself."

Brigadier General Daniel H. Reynolds had been in the act of moving his Confederate brigade at this moment, and he tried to stop the fleeing horde. But, wrote Gale, "Not a man would stop! The First Tennessee came by, and its colonel, House, was the only man who would stop with us, and finding none of his men willing to stand, he too went on his way." All seemed lost. Gale sent a message to Stewart "that he might save himself." A few minutes later Gale galloped where he expected to find Hood and Stewart. "They were gone and in their places the Yankees. I turned my horse's head toward the steep knobs and spurred away."

On the Federal far left, at Overton Hill, General Wood's troops were regrouping on the lower slopes after their failed attack against Stephen Lee's Confederates. Suddenly Wood's men heard a great roar erupting at the other side of the Federal line, and they understood what it meant — their comrades had broken through. It was, Corporal George Herr wrote, "a sea of sound pealing from the right — the measureless roar of thousands of human voices raised in exultant paens of victory it was magnetic, it electrified the men." Corporal Herr remembered that the Federals at Overton Hill turned around with hardly a word and charged the lines from which they had just retreated "with an elan that was as irresistible as mysterious. It rushed forward like a mighty wave, driving everything before it." The Federals overran Lee's lines, but the Confederates refused to be routed. They gave ground slowly and in

good order. Then Lee looked to his left, in the direction of Shy's Hill, and saw the collapse rippling toward him.

He galloped wildly toward the break, his horse taking fences in all-out stride, and reined up in a churning mob. A color-bearer passed and Lee snatched the standard from the man's hands and waved it dramatically overhead as his horse wheeled. "Rally, men, rally!" he cried hoarsely. "For God's sake, rally! This is the place for brave men to die!"

Somehow he succeeded, stopping enough men to gain control of the situation and prevent the panic from infecting his own corps. "The effect was electrical," one soldier wrote. "Men gathered in little knots of four or five and he soon had around him three or four other stands of colors." A few pieces of artillery joined Lee, "and a little drummer boy who beat the long roll in perfect time."

On the demolished Confederate left, meanwhile, General Reynolds had managed to keep his 1st Arkansas Mounted Rifles intact. He placed them in the path of the advancing Federals and thus helped General Cheatham to save what remained of Hood's left from capture. When the last of the friendly troops passed through his ranks, Reynolds started his brigade down the muddy road toward Franklin and left the rear guard to the cavalry.

It now was near dark, and the advancing Federal infantrymen paused as they approached the remnants of Confederate resistance along the escape routes leading south. Most Federal units stopped for the night.

But the Federal cavalry remained active. Through the darkness came Wilson's troopers, now remounted and on the gallop. The cavalrymen crashed ahead until they ran into a stout barricade just west of the Franklin

Pike, behind which a rear guard of dismounted cavalry under James Chalmers waited. The rain was turning into sleet as some of the hardest fighting commenced. In the darkness the troopers clashed hand to hand, with pistol and saber, close and brutal.

One of the Federal cavalry regiments was the 12th Tennessee, under Colonel George Spaulding. During the fray Spaulding collided with someone who shouted, "Who are you, anyhow?" Spaulding identified himself and the other man seized the reins of his horse, crying, "Well, you are my prisoner, for I am Colonel Ed Rucker, commanding the 12th Tennessee Rebel Cavalry!"

"Not by a damned sight," said Spaulding, slashing with his saber and spurring his horse. Just then Captain Joseph C. Boy-

In a photograph taken December 16, a few troops linger south of Nashville in the outer line of Federal works, recently abandoned by the main force pushing south against Hood. Campfires still smolder in the distance in the midst of a litter of timber, felled to provide fuel, shelter and fortifications.

er of the Federal 12th Tennessee closed with Rucker. Boyer managed to snatch away Rucker's saber — just as Rucker seized his. They fought with exchanged sabers until a pistol shot broke Rucker's sword arm and he was compelled to surrender.

Sheer numbers finally forced the Confederate rear guard to withdraw, and Chalmers' troopers went south along the now empty road, having seen the last of Hood's army move to safety. While the Union troops milled about, Wilson heard hoofbeats on the road behind him. A heavy figure loomed, and he recognized General Thomas' voice.

In a roar of triumph that Wilson thought could be heard for a quarter mile, the usually reserved and dignified Thomas cried, "Dang it to hell, Wilson, didn't I tell you we could lick 'em, didn't I tell you we could lick 'em?"

Later that night, John Bell Hood was sitting alone in his headquarters. A soldier remembered, "He was much agitated and affected, pulling his hair with one hand (he had but one) and crying like his heart would break."

The battle of Nashville was over. It had cost the Union about 3,000 men killed, wounded and missing; the Confederates estimated their losses at 6,400. The outcome of the contest had never been in question — just the matter of how long the Confederate soldiers would continue to fight impossible odds. Exhausted, freezing, hungry and hopeless, they nevertheless fought on as long as bone and muscle and heart could endure.

The Army of Tennessee was finished as a fighting force, and the war in the west was nearly over. Hood led his beaten, demoralized men back to Franklin and on toward the Tennessee River, followed all the way by Wilson's vigorous cavalry. Forrest had re-

joined Hood's troops on December 19 and did his best to hold off the Federals, but it was to no avail. The Confederates crossed the Tennessee two days after Christmas. When Thomas' pursuing troops reached the river, he decided to call off the chase. Hood's army would never fight again. On January 13, 1865, Hood asked to be relieved of command. Ten days later, President Jefferson Davis complied with the request.

Meanwhile, as this desperate denouement unfolded in Tennessee, Sherman and his army of 62,000 men were marching along on what was proving to be an extended holiday, bearing down on Savannah. It was all stunningly unwarlike. The grime of war was far behind them and they strode along examining the new sights.

"The weather was fine, the roads good and everything seemed to favor us," Sherman wrote. "Never do I recall a more agreeable sensation than the sight of our camps by night lit up by the fire of fragrant pine-knots. No enemy opposed us, and we could only occasionally hear the faint reverberation of a gun to our left rear, where Kilpatrick was skirmishing with Wheeler's cavalry."

The soil was sandy in these Georgia low-lands, and more and more often the men encountered swamps and flooded rice fields. Since corn was scarce, the men were reduced to eating rice. It was a new grain for most of them, and many went hungry until they learned to hull it. Still, they were within a dozen miles of the oyster beds, and a bit farther beyond, Navy supply ships. Until then, as an Ohio colonel told his men, "the only thing I can advise is to draw in your belts one more hole each day."

The ground grew steadily more marshy

until it was unrelieved swamp. The marchers began to encounter opposition, though it was more courageous than effective. Here and there handfuls of intrepid Confederates had built emplacements; some were substantial, but others were mere depressions hastily scraped out behind newly felled trees. In any case, the approaching army scarcely paused in sweeping the enemy aside. The lead brigade of each advancing column simply sent a regiment to each side of the obstacle, taking it in flank. Sherman's staff officer, Major Henry Hitchcock, described one of these works as "merely small earth banks running thirty yards or less into swamp on either side of the road."

But as the army neared the fixed defenses of Savannah, the opposition grew more seri-ous. On one occasion a persistent Confederate gun began to bang away at the marchers, and Sherman walked forward in a railroad cut to get a better look. "Very soon," as he wrote later, "I saw the white puff of smoke, and, watching close, caught sight of the ball as it rose in its flight, and finding it coming pretty straight, I stepped a short distance to one side." A watching soldier saw the shot too: "It grows, It is as large as a tincup—as a plate—a barrel. Now its immensity fills the entire field of vision, shutting out the sky." It sounded like "a steam engine starting," another man said, beginning with a whiffling noise "and ending with a roar." Then, Sherman said, "the ball (a 32-pound round shot) struck the ground, and rose in its first ricochet, caught a Federal soldier under the right

Smoke billowing from their stacks, four Confederate transports approach a pair of closely moored Federal vessels on the Savannah River in November 1864 to pick up sick and wounded Confederate prisoners as part of a general exchange of invalid captives. After this mission of mercy, the Confederate steamer *Ida (center)* resumed her role as flagship of the Savannah River Squadron, only to be disabled by Sherman's artillery on December 10 and destroyed.

jaw, and literally carried away his head, scattering blood and brains." Recalled Hitchcock, "The General wisely concluded to leave, and we all rode back up road ¼ mile."

Five causeways ran into the city across the marshes, canals and flooded rice fields that lay between the Savannah River on Sherman's left and the Ogeechee River on his right. The Confederates held fast to the east bank of the Savannah — the South Carolina side — denying the Federals access to that waterway. The Union troops splashed for-

ward through the marshes until they reached the city's defenses, a trench line with earthworks and rifle pits protected by sharpened stakes, lying behind rice fields in which water could be raised or lowered by floodgates. Before this truly formidable barrier, the Federal troops paused and formed a siege line in an irregular crescent. They were about four miles from Savannah proper; church bells could be heard when the wind was right. The weather turned cold, and in the swampy terrain the men were rarely dry.

A sketch drawn after the fall of Savannah shows the formidable barrier that faced Sherman west of the city — a sturdy parapet notched with artillery embrasures and bordered by a swamp. "It will be hard work in our front," one Federal wrote in mid-December. "But if we make a start we are going through and I think the Johnnys know it for they do not talk as saucy as they did at Vicksburg."

An Illinois captain remembered crossing a canal at night, plunging to his armpits. "Our bones were fairly frozen," he wrote, "and the marrow within them congealed."

By December 12, Sherman had deployed his forces between the Ogeechee and the Savannah Rivers, facing Savannah's defenses.

"We had again run up against the old familiar parapet, with its deep ditches, canals and bayous full of water," Sherman wrote, "and it looked as though another siege was inevitable." He was near his goal, but he was not safe, for he faced an enemy in place and he had yet to reach the sea and make contact with the U.S. Navy.

Sherman's men knew they were facing a fight now. The young 100th Indiana soldier Theodore Upson recalled the gun captain of a nearby embrasure telling him and his comrades to lie low. "He was going to wake up the Johnnys," Upson wrote. "He fired both of his guns. He woke them up all right. They replied, knocked the muzzle off the gun next to us, the wheel of the other, blew up the caisson and threw one shell into the muck in front of us which exploded and covered us with about 20 tons of black mud."

In Washington, President Lincoln continued to wait anxiously, as he had for weeks, for news of the army marching across Georgia. The suspense felt so intensely in the White House was shared by the public as newspapers counted the days since Sherman had cut the telegraph link to the North and disappeared. Grant, in Virginia facing Lee's army in stalemate, waited impatiently for his old friend "to come out at salt water," not unaware that his own career was on the line with Sherman's. The Navy was hanging offshore, steaming regularly up the Ogeechee just out of range of the Confederate defenses

and hurling signal rockets into the night. There had been no response from Sherman.

The fate of Sherman and his army was never far from President Lincoln's mind. Senator John Sherman of Ohio asked him at a White House meeting if there was word of his brother. "Oh, no," said Lincoln, "I know the hole he went in at, but I can't tell you what hole he'll come out of." Later Lincoln asked a friend, "Wouldn't you like to hear something from Sherman?" Expecting news, the man brightened. Lincoln laughed. "Well, I'll be hanged if I wouldn't myself." Lincoln's preoccupation was pervasive; a guest, finding the President ignoring him in a reception line, demanded recognition. Lincoln apologized and said: "I was thinking of a man down south."

On another occasion the President attempted to get a message to Sherman via Colonel A. H. Markland, who was leaving Washington with mail for Sherman's army. At the White House, Lincoln took Mark-

Brigadier General William B. Hazen (*left*), called on to lead the dangerous assault on Fort McAllister (*below*) near the mouth of the Ogeechee River, met the task coolly. About 4 p.m. on December 13, his corps commander reported, Hazen sounded the advance and "the brave men rushed through a line of torpedoes and heavy abatis, jumped into the wide and deep ditch, and climbed in one heroic élan, which secured them the fort after a few minutes' struggle, but not without a heavy loss."

land's hand. "Say to him, for me, 'God bless him and God bless his army.' That is as much as I can say and more than I can write." Markland remembered tears in the President's eyes. Departing, Markland heard the President call to him. "When I looked back, he was standing like a statue where I had left him. 'Now, remember what I say. God bless Sherman and all his army.' "

Inside Savannah, meanwhile, General William Hardee was rallying what troops he could muster. His earthworks were strong and studded with artillery, but his men numbered scarcely 10,000. Among them were the remnants of the Georgia militia that had suffered such bloody losses against Sherman's rear guard at Griswoldville.

Since then, the militiamen had seen action. In late November, Federal troops had tried to seize the railroad that ran from the South Carolina side of the Savannah River north to Charleston. They had started from Port Royal, a small Union enclave on the South Carolina coast captured in 1861.

When the Federal advance began, Hardee and Lieutenant General Richard E. Taylor, who had been together at Macon, were gravely concerned. The railroad was their sole route of withdrawal to Charleston. If they lost it, Hardee's whole force, such as it was, would be trapped in Savannah when Sherman arrived.

It happened that the battered militiamen under Major General Gustavus Smith reached Savannah on the day that the Federals were approaching the railroad. As soon as Smith's troops got there, Smith hustled them over to the South Carolina side of the river. The militiamen took careful position along a causeway and hurled back the Federal advance. The fighting was a reverse of

their last bloody encounter with Sherman — they inflicted 10 casualties for each one of their own and kept open Hardee's railroad escape route into South Carolina.

Beauregard, still in overall command, arrived in Savannah just before Sherman's troops pulled up before the city's defensive perimeter. Beauregard told Hardee not to risk capture of his own army, which would be needed if Sherman moved into South Carolina. Instead, Hardee should start building a pontoon bridge to evacuate his men across the mile-wide river to safety.

As for Sherman, his prime concern was to link up with the Navy. But he could not use the Savannah as an avenue to the sea

because the Confederates held both banks in strength. The way down the Ogeechee, moreover, was blocked by Fort McAllister, which stood on the south bank, guns fixed on the river entrance from Ossabaw Sound. Navy vessels had steamed close enough to the fort daily to draw its fire. Approximately 200 Confederate gunners manned the fort, and it indeed appeared formidable.

Kilpatrick's cavalrymen had tested the fort and had judged it too strong for the troopers to take. But Major General Oliver O. Howard, the commander of Sherman's south wing, deemed Fort McAllister vulnerable to infantry assault. The one-armed general volunteered to reduce it and sent Brigadier General William B. Hazen's division forward to launch the assault. This was Sherman's old outfit; he had led it to victory at Shiloh and Vicksburg and he knew what it could do. Sherman told Hazen that the safety of the whole army and the success of the campaign rested on him. Then on December 13, as Hazen deployed his troops for the attack, Sherman rode to the Cheeves plantation three miles upriver from the fort. He and Howard climbed onto a lookout platform built on the roof of the house. Through his field glass, Sherman saw Hazen's men pause at the edge of a forest. He immediately sent orders to hurry the assault. "The sun was rapidly declining," Sherman wrote later, "and I was dreadfully impatient."

At that very moment a steamer with tall black stacks slid into view well below the fort. At last — it was the Navy. A signal flag flashed from the ship's bow with a question:

"Who are you?"

"General Sherman," came the reply from the lookout perch.

"Is Fort McAllister taken?"

"Not yet, but it will be in a minute!"

Just then there was a roll of fire from the direction of the fort. Sherman later recalled the action that unfolded: "We saw Hazen's troops come out of the dark fringe of woods, the lines dressed as on parade, colors flying, and moving forward with a quick steady pace. Fort McAllister was then all alive, its big guns belching forth dense clouds of smoke, which soon enveloped our assaulting lines. One color went down but was up in a moment."

Hitchcock entered in his journal the account of a man who was watching with Sherman: "The column dashed against the lunette, some 20 flags in line. Straight forward they pressed on to the main work but presently the head of column seemed to sink down and disappear. The General had been watching them through his field glass with eager anxiety but when this apparent hesitation — the sign of ruinous repulse if real — appeared, he took down his glass as if unable to witness the failure." Then the column reappeared, "still pressing forward, and in another minute had reached and was on the parapet — the Fort was ours!"

Sherman was ecstatic. "I've got Savannah!" he cried gleefully. He sent an exuberant message to General Slocum: "Take a good big drink, a long breath and then yell like the devil. The fort was carried at 4:30 p.m., the assault lasting but fifteen minutes."

Hurriedly Sherman found a small boat and rowed down to the fort as night fell, his younger officers at the oars. General Hazen was waiting to report losses of 92 killed and wounded. "Inside the fort lay the dead as they had fallen," Sherman wrote, "and they could hardly be distinguished from their liv-

A Federal work party in captured Fort McAllister prepares to winch a Columbiad from its carriage for use elsewhere against the Confederates. Twenty-four guns were taken in the assault on the fort, along with 40 tons of ammunition and a month's supply of food for the garrison.

The Confederacy's Infernal Machines

As William Hazen's Federals prepared to attack Fort McAllister, they faced a chilling array of defenses: felled trees, stout palisades and a parapet bristling with cannon. But a greater threat went unseen, for the Confederates had salted the ground around the fort with land mines — or torpedoes, as they were then known. In the charge, Hazen noted grimly, a host of these devices were touched off by the "tread of the troops, blowing many men to atoms." Torpedoes caused most of the Federal casualties there.

The mining of Fort McAllister was not an isolated incident. At the urging of President Jefferson Davis himself, many roads and causeways leading to Savannah had been mined. And while relatively few Federals ran afoul of these so-called infernal machines, the explosions had an unnerving impact. As one Federal engineer wrote, the torpedoes worked "as much by their moral effect as by actual destruction of life."

That the Confederates had such a weapon in their arsenal was due in large part to the efforts of Brigadier General Gabriel Rains of North Carolina. A pioneer in the development of the land mine, he had tested his first device in 1840 against the Seminole Indians in Florida, where he was serving as a captain in the Regular Army. The debut proved less than auspicious: Planted near a pond frequented by Seminole warriors, the torpedo claimed a victim; but when Rains and his men got there they were ambushed, and the inventor himself was shot.

Recovering, Rains pressed on with his work, and by the outbreak of the Civil War he had evolved two triggering mechanisms for his torpedoes: a friction primer, set off by a trip wire that acted like the lanyard on a cannon; and the pressure-sensitive fuse shown here, rigged to detonate when struck by an object exerting at least seven pounds of pressure.

Though Federals and Confederates alike protested the adoption of such blindly impersonal weapons, Rains won the backing of the War Department in Richmond and in 1864 was named head of the Torpedo Bureau. Confronted with the fruits of Rains's efforts in Georgia that summer, Sherman reacted with accustomed severity. Near Atlanta in June he advised a subordinate that if the officer suspected the presence of torpedoes in the path, he should test the ground with "a car-load of prisoners, or citizens implicated, drawn by a long rope." And in December, outside Savannah, Sherman ordered some Confederate prisoners to clear torpedoes from a road. Two of the captives begged to be let off, a Federal officer recalled. But Sherman was adamant, saying that Confederates had placed the mines to assassinate his men and that if Confederates "got blown up he didn't care." At this, the officer wrote, Sherman's hostages set to the task, retrieving the torpedoes *very carefully* — and without accident."

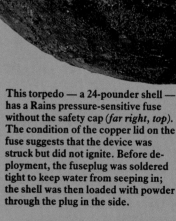

BRIGADIER GENERAL GABRIEL RAINS

This torpedo — a 24-pounder shell — has a Rains pressure-sensitive fuse without the safety cap (*far right, top*). The condition of the copper lid on the fuse suggests that the device was struck but did not ignite. Before deployment, the fuseplug was soldered tight to keep water from seeping in; the shell was then loaded with powder through the plug in the side.

Toiling by the palisade of Fort McAllister after its capture by the Federals, Confederate prisoners dig up unexploded torpedoes at the insistence of their guards — a practice endorsed by General Sherman. The former Confederate commander of the fort, Major George Anderson, protested, terming such perilous duty "unwarrantable and improper."

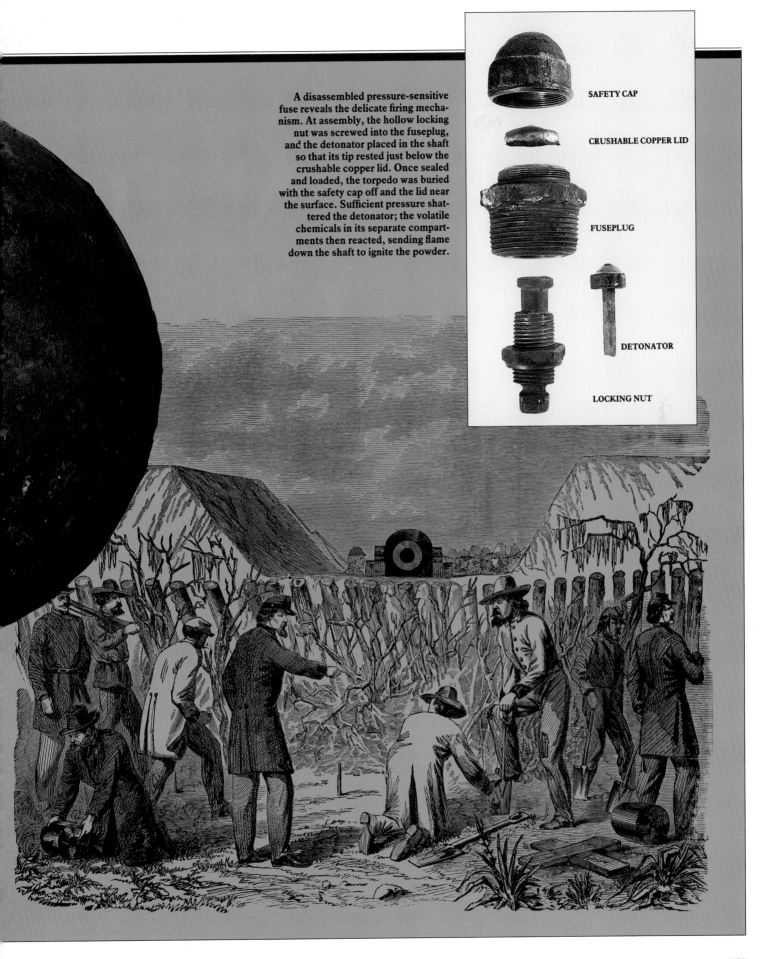

A disassembled pressure-sensitive fuse reveals the delicate firing mechanism. At assembly, the hollow locking nut was screwed into the fuseplug, and the detonator placed in the shaft so that its tip rested just below the crushable copper lid. Once sealed and loaded, the torpedo was buried with the safety cap off and the lid near the surface. Sufficient pressure shattered the detonator; the volatile chemicals in its separate compartments then reacted, sending flame down the shaft to ignite the powder.

SAFETY CAP

CRUSHABLE COPPER LID

FUSEPLUG

DETONATOR

LOCKING NUT

At top, Union soldiers on the bank of the Ogeechee River hail the appearance of the U.S. Navy near Fort McAllister on December 13. Flag signals from the tug *Dandelion*, above, established communication with Sherman on the shore. From a distance, Sherman thought the vessel was a gunboat and asked if it could assist in the attack on the fort. "No heavy guns aboard," the *Dandelion's* commander signaled back.

ing comrades, sleeping soundly side by side in the pale moonlight."

Later that night, Sherman boarded a yawl and sailed toward Ossabaw Sound. The yawl pulled alongside a vessel at anchor. Its officers welcomed aboard the general for whom they had waited so long, and he scrawled a report to Secretary of War Stanton that ended: "I regard Savannah as already *gained*." Major General John G. Foster, commander of the Federal enclave at Port Royal, was on board a ship nearby and soon gave Sherman good news: A full division of fresh troops awaited him at Port Royal, a mere 20 miles up the coast, with mountains of supplies that would begin moving in the morning.

The next day Sherman reached the flagship of Admiral John A. Dahlgren, commander of the South Atlantic Blockading Squadron. Sailors hung from the yards and cheered as he came aboard, which delighted him. As he shook hands with the admiral he seemed overwhelmed with pleasure — and, perhaps, with relief. He had marched across Georgia and had linked up with the Navy. The capture of Savannah was only a matter of time. Sherman strode about talking in his most intense manner, fingers snapping, eyes glowing, clouds of cigar smoke billowing around him. "I've got Savannah," he boomed. "It's in my grip." When Sherman finally started back to his troops, a young Navy officer who had been near him on the ship confided that he "felt it a relief and experienced almost an exhaustion after the excitement of his vigorous presence."

On December 15 — the day that Thomas launched his attack at Nashville — Sherman returned to his army and ordered Generals Slocum and Howard to prepare the troops for an assault on Savannah. Colonel Markland arrived that day with the mail, just as a

A hobbled Major General John Foster, commander of the Federal Department of the South, clasps the hand of General Sherman as he boards the steamer *Nemaha* early on December 14. The aide who summoned Sherman to this conference from occupied Fort McAllister (*background*) explained that Foster had aggravated an old Mexican War wound and could not come ashore.

load of fresh rations came in from Port Royal. He delivered Lincoln's message.

"I thank the President," Sherman responded. "Say my army is all right."

The troops were delighted by the unexpected and long overdue arrival of mail. "Such cheering I never heard," said a Minnesota corporal. Markland described it as "a frantic sight, men snatching letters, whooping at this first touch with home." An Illinois man remembered the soldiers "reading their letters held in one hand while devouring hard-tack from the other." But it was a sad day for young Theodore Upson. One letter said his parents were losing the farm and another that his girl back home was dying. "I am all broke up," Upson wrote in his journal. "It just seems as though the bottom was falling out of everything I just cannot bear to think of it."

Grant's aide, Lieutenant Colonel Orville E. Babcock, also arrived with a message for Sherman from his chief. Sherman ripped the letter open outside his headquarters and began to read. His own aide, Captain Lewis M. Dayton, saw Sherman "make that nervous motion of the left arm which characterized him when anything annoyed him, as if he was pushing something away from him."

"Come here, Dayton," Sherman snapped. Inside his headquarters, the general began to swear and cried out, "Won't do it; I won't do anything of the kind!"

The gist of Grant's message was most unwelcome. He wanted Sherman to bring his army to Virginia by ship and join the Army of the Potomac in defeating Robert E. Lee at Petersburg. But Sherman had counted on continuing his triumphant march into South Carolina, and he was enraged at the thought of being thwarted. Shipping 62,000 men to

Virginia would take nearly as long as marching them there, and Sherman knew that the impact of his swath across Georgia would be magnified tenfold if he could lay waste with fire and sword through the state that was the cradle of the rebellion. Why, Grant's idea did not even envision Sherman's pausing to pluck the ripe plum of Savannah.

For an hour or more Sherman fumed. Then he took control of himself. Of course he would obey Grant's orders, but he would also write impassioned defenses of his Carolina plan. It would take some time to gather ships; while waiting, he would go ahead and capture Savannah.

Still, Sherman hesitated to act until his men had corduroyed roads against the coming winter rains and he had brought in siege guns from Port Royal. Savannah's defenders could make the cost of taking the city very expensive if they chose. A heavy casualty list at the end of his successful march was the last thing Sherman wanted. As a trial shot, then, he sent Hardee an ultimatum: Surrender immediately, or the Federal commander would "feel justified in resorting to the harshest measures, and shall make little effort to restrain my army." Hardee gave him a dignified refusal, expressing distaste for his enemy's crudeness.

Whereupon, Sherman noted later, "nothing remained but to assault." He decided to make one more preliminary move: He would bring Foster's small division from Port Royal to occupy the Carolina bank of the Savannah River, facing the city. This would "completely surround Savannah on all sides, so as further to excite Hardee's fears, and in case of success, to capture the whole of his army."

The tricky part was that Foster's little force would be vulnerable to attack when it

A Captive's Lyrical Tribute

Word that Sherman was descending on Savannah spread swiftly through the South, instilling fear in many but cheering others with the prospect of deliverance. Adjutant Samuel Byers of the 5th Iowa was languishing in a prison camp in Columbia, South Carolina, when he learned of Sherman's exploits. As Byers wrote later, he owed this intelligence to "an old negro, who was permitted to come in and sell us a little bread." Asked for news of the War, the old man soon complied "by secreting a copy of the morning paper inside a loaf of bread. It did not tell much, but between its troubled lines I saw that Sherman's boys were overwhelming everything and hurrying to the coast."

The discovery inspired Byers to verse. Huddled on a pile of straw under his old Army blanket, he penned a tribute in five stanzas to Sherman and his men that celebrated their progress from the "wild hills of Resaca" to "Atlanta's grim walls" — and thence to the sea. The poem was set to music by another inmate and performed by a group of captives on the steps of the prison hospital. What the guards thought of this performance is not known, but the song, "When Sherman Marched down to the Sea," was destined to take the Union by storm.

Smuggled North early in 1865, Byers' song was distributed by at least a dozen publishers; in time more than a million copies were sold. Yet the reception Byers valued most came from an audience of one. Shortly before the Federals reached Columbia in February, Byers escaped, and as Sherman rode into the city the composer caught his attention and gave him a copy of the song. Charmed, the general put Byers on his staff. After the War, Sherman would remark that Byers' song had given new meaning to the campaign, investing a long and often laborious "change of base" with the "glamour of romance."

Federal officer Samuel Byers — shown at right in civilian dress — wrote in captivity this draft of the popular song, "When Sherman Marched down to the Sea." The original was taken North by a paroled prisoner, who hid it in his wooden leg.

moved, since the main Federal army would have to cross the river to come to its rescue. Sherman chose to go personally to Port Royal to explain just what he wanted. In the city, meanwhile, time was running out. Defense now seemed hopeless and loomed as a potential waste of troops who might be invaluable in South Carolina. Beauregard returned for an inspection. It was December 16, the day — though no word of it would come through — that Hood's army was finally destroyed at Nashville. Much to Beauregard's irritation, the pontoon bridge across the Savannah River was unfinished; he tongue-lashed the engineers so vigorously that in three days the escape route was ready. The engineers used well-caulked rice boats from nearby plantations for pontoons, said Lieutenant Colonel Alexander Chisolm, Beauregard's aide. "These, moored by old guns and car wheels for anchors, were covered with flooring supplied by pulling down the wharves and wooden buildings."

In heavy fog on the night of December 20, while Sherman was still off arranging Foster's move and the Federal army lay quiet with orders to initiate no offensive action, Hardee laid down a bombardment to conceal

his movement and began his escape. A detail stayed behind to keep the campfires bright, as unit after unit crossed the pontoon bridge into South Carolina.

At least some of the watching Federal troops knew what was happening. "I think our officers knew they were going and did not try to stop them," Upson recalled, "for we could hear them all night moving about and most of us think we might have cut them off and captured the whole of them." But, he added, "I am awfully glad we did not have to charge their works."

Private Horatio Chapman of the 20th Connecticut was in an advanced position. When the Confederate bombardment ended about midnight, Chapman dozed off. Sometime later he awakened with a start. The Confederate lines were silent and a single white flag was in view. He called his lieutenant and the two went cautiously forward. They found two wounded Confederates under the flag. "They're all gone but us. They pulled out in a big hurry."

By dawn of December 21, the last of the Confederates had crossed. They cut loose the pontoon bridge and let it drift downriver against the shore. A day later Sherman

Hardee's Confederates file across a pontoon bridge over the Savannah River, retreating from the city to the South Carolina shore on December 20. That evening, before abandoning the works west of town to join in this evacuation, a regimental band struck up "Dixie," prompting a Federal in the distance to jeer: "Played out!"

Torched by her crew to keep her out of enemy hands, the Confederate ram *Savannah* explodes shortly before dawn on December 21 as a factory burns in the foreground. The eruption shook buildings in nearby Savannah, which a few hours later would pass quietly to the Federals.

returned to find his troops in Savannah.

The city was quiet. The Confederates had laid waste to their navy yard and an ironclad was still burning, but everything else was intact. Taken with the city were 250 heavy guns and 31,000 bales of valuable cotton. Sherman was irritated a day or two later to learn that a Treasury agent, A. G. Browne, was in the city to claim that cotton. When Sherman called Browne in, the agent made a happy suggestion: Why not offer Lincoln the city for Christmas?

So on Christmas Eve, Lincoln received a wire, drafted before the tally of booty was complete: "I beg to present you, as a Christmas gift, the city of Savannah, with 150 heavy guns and plenty of ammunition, and also about 25,000 bales of cotton."

On Christmas morning Lincoln released the text, and it swept across the country — a gift for a weary nation.

At the same time, Sherman received good news. Grant reversed himself. He told Sherman not to leave for Virginia — the army was to march across South Carolina, just as its general had proposed. Sherman intended to deliver the coup de grâce to the Confederacy.

With complete satisfaction, he wrote of his stay in Savannah: "Here terminated the 'March to the Sea.'" Surely he had the right to be proud. The army that he had left in Tennessee under Thomas, the commander he had chosen, had destroyed Hood's army and all but ended the war in the west. And Sherman himself had brought off an epic march. He had confounded the military critics, led his men 275 miles across the Southern heartland and brought them to Savannah in better condition than when they started. Most important, he had lived up to his aim: He had laid waste to Georgia. "The destruction could hardly have been worse," one of his men said, "if Atlanta had been a volcano in eruption and the molten lava had flowed in a stream 60 miles wide and five times as long."

It was a triumph that would become an indelible part of United States legend. But it had not been easy, and no one knew this better than the man who had conceived it and carried it out at the risk of his reputation. "Like a man who has walked a narrow plank," he wrote his wife, "I look back and wonder if I really did it."

Savannah in Defeat

Approaching Savannah early on December 21, 1864, the advance guard of General Sherman's army got an unexpected reception. Mayor Richard Arnold welcomed the invading troops and conducted them to the city center. The mayor, who four years earlier had vowed "war to the knife, and the knife to the hilt," now swallowed his pride and surrendered the port city of 20,000 without a shot having to be fired.

The mayor's decision was accepted by most of the city's war-weary citizens. Some Savannah residents took detours to avoid walking under the Stars and Stripes, however, and an Episcopal clergyman neglected the customary prayer for the President at Christmas services. But many families opened their homes — if not their hearts —

to Union officers and charmed them with gracious Southern manners.

General Sherman, anxious to counter his image as a "Vandal Chief," responded in kind. He kept his troops out of trouble with a succession of drills, inspections and parades. Moreover, he tactfully ignored orders issued by the War Department that instructed him to deport all diehard se-

cessionists and arm newly freed slaves.

Yet Sherman's conciliatory efforts were soon undone. After his departure from Savannah on January 21, 1865, families with strong Confederate ties were gradually banished by order of the Union occupiers. And three regiments of black troops arrived to guard the city, bringing home the reality of defeat to Savannah's proud citizens.

Savannah Ga. Dec 22. 1864
Via Ft. Monroe Va Dec 25.

His Excellency
Prest. Lincoln.
    I beg to present you as a
Christmas gift the city of Savannah
with 150 heavy guns & plenty
of ammunition & also about
25.000 bales of cotton.
    W. T. Sherman
        major Genl

In a Savannah parlor freshly bedecked with the Stars and Stripes, General Sherman (*standing*) toasts his staff at a Christmas dinner. The Union victory celebration was enhanced by the largess of some of Savannah's leading citizens, who donated fine wines and the use of this well-appointed mansion.

General Sherman and staff (*center*) review Federal regiments marching down Savannah's Bay Street. Sherman missed the city's surrender on December 21 because the warship he was aboard grounded on a mudbank. Arriving the next day, he wrote the jubilant message (*top*) that was telegraphed to President Lincoln.

SAVANNAH DAILY

"REDEEMED, REGENERATED AND DISENTHRALLED

BY M SUMMERS, CAPT. A. Q. M.

SAVANNAH, GEORGIA, SATU

DAILY LOYAL GEORGIAN.

SATURDAY EVENING, DECEMBER 24, 1864.

HEADQ'RS CITY OF SAVANNAH,
December 23, 1864.

GENERAL ORDERS,
No. 1.

In accordance with orders received, the undersigned has assumed command of the city. The following Staff Officers are announced:

Capt. W. T. FORBES, A. A. A. G. and Chief of Staff.

Capt. S. B. WHEELOCK, A. A. A. G.

UNION VICTORY.

GREAT BATTLE IN FRONT OF NASHVILLE, TENN.

Rebel Army Driven back over Three Miles.

	Weig
BUSHELS.	
Wheat	
Shelled Cor	
Corn in the	
Peas	
Rye	
Oats	
Barley	
Irish Potat	
Sweet Potat	
White Bean	

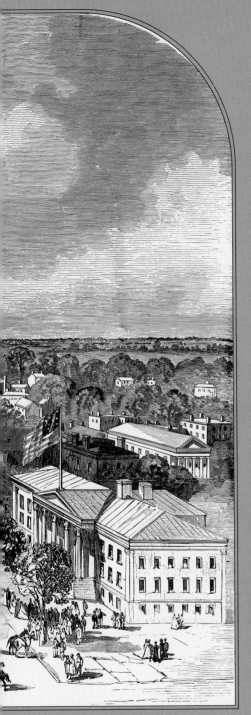

Savannah residents look on as occupation forces parade down the unscathed waterfront. Although rearguard Confederates were burning cotton bales on the east side of the river, raising trails of smoke on the horizon (*left*), they avoided shelling the city for fear of harming civilians.

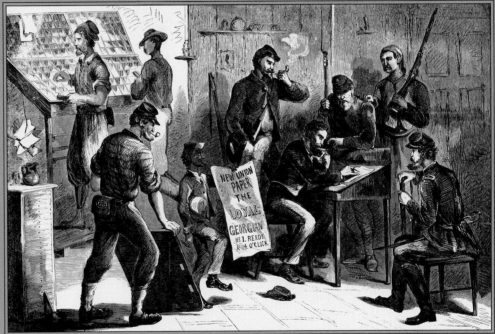

In offices requisitioned from the Savannah *News*, a pro-Union editor puts his own slant on events as typesetters prepare the first issue of the *Daily Loyal Georgian* (*bottom*). With censorship in effect, readers were given breathless accounts of Union advances and Confederate retreats.

LOYAL GEORGIAN

HE UNION, IT MUST AND SHALL BE PRESERVED!"

Y EVENING, DECEMBER 24, 1864　　　**VOL. 1.---NO. 1.**

Racing to remove obstructions near the mouth of the Savannah River, Federal work crews pry apart wooden cribs — filled with paving stones and caked with river silt — that blocked supply ships *(background)*.

With the channel cleared, Union ships at the Savannah wharf are loaded with a harvest of confiscated cotton that the retreating Confederates failed to destroy. Sherman shipped $30 million worth of it to New York.

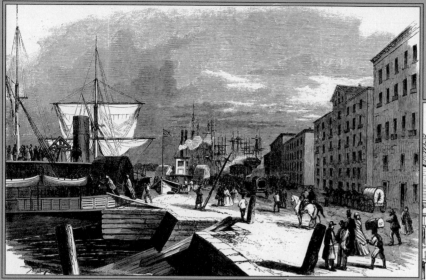

Offered free passage to Charleston, families of Confederate officers board a Union steamer at Savannah in January 1865. Sherman, who had been the guest of some of these families during a prewar visit, had arranged the transport under a flag of truce for those who wanted to join their menfolk in South Carolina.

Savannah's rich and poor mingle as they line up for handouts of flour, salt and bacon, part of a relief shipment donated by the citizens of Boston and New York. With wheat flour selling for $125 a sack before the occupation, and grits going for $16 a bushel, many of the seaport's citizens had taken to eating boiled shrimp for breakfast.

Union soldiers gather outside Savannah townhouses, whose matrons earned needed cash by baking and selling sweet corncakes. "Those Yankees all want something sweet," reasoned one lady, "and we want some greenbacks."

167

With flames spreading behind them,
Union soldiers haul a wagonload of
shells away from a great fire that
spread terror through Savannah on
January 27, 1865. The fire raged for
18 hours, destroying 200 houses
and narrowly missing an arsenal
packed with 60 tons of gunpowder.

Exploding shells hurl deadly fragments through the air, piercing a water tower and forcing city fire fighters
to abandon their equipment and flee.
The cause of the conflagration was
never determined; Unionists suspected a Confederate saboteur, while
most residents blamed the Federals.

ACKNOWLEDGMENTS

The editors wish to thank the following individuals and institutions for their valuable assistance in the preparation of this volume:

Georgia: Atlanta — Thomas Dickey.

Indiana: Notre Dame — Charles Lamb, University of Notre Dame Archives.

Iowa: Des Moines — Mark Peitzman, Iowa State Historical Museum.

Maryland: Hyattsville — Mark Meader.

Ohio: Columbus — Tauni Graham, Ohio Historical Society; Larry M. Strayer. Lancaster — Laura Kerr; Phyllis Kuhn, Fairfield Heritage Association.

Pennsylvania: Carlisle — Randy Hackenberg, Michael J. Winey, U.S. Army Military History Institute.

Virginia: Falls Church — Christopher Nelson. McLean — Charles H. Jones Jr. Petersburg — Sergei Troubetzkoy, Siege Museum. Quantico — Tony Tommell.

Washington, D.C.: Michael R. Harris, Smithsonian Institution; Eveline Nave, Library of Congress Photoduplication Service.

Wisconsin: Madison — Dr. Gregory Higby, American Institute of the History of Pharmacy.

The index was prepared by Roy Nanovic.

BIBLIOGRAPHY

Books

Belknap, Charles Eugene, *Recollections of a Bummer.* Lansing, Mich.: R. Smith Printing Co., 1898.

Bennett, L. G., and Wm. M. Haigh, *History of the Thirty-Sixth Regiment Illinois Volunteers: During the War of the Rebellion.* Aurora, Ill.: Knickerbocker & Hodder, 1876.

Board of Commissioners, *Minnesota in the Civil and Indian Wars: 1861-1865.* St. Paul: Pioneer Press Co., 1890.

Boatner, Mark Mayo, III, *The Civil War Dictionary.* New York: David McKay Co., 1959.

Bowman, S. M., and R. B. Irwin, *Sherman and His Campaigns: A Military Biography.* New York: Charles B. Richardson, 1865.

Bradley, G. S., *The Star Corps: or, Notes of an Army Chaplain, during Sherman's Famous "March to the Sea."* Milwaukee: Jermain & Brightman, 1865.

Brock, R. A., ed., *Southern Historical Society Papers.* Vols. 18 and 24. Millwood, N.Y.: Kraus Reprint, 1977 (reprint of 1890 edition).

Brooks, Stewart, *Civil War Medicine.* Springfield, Ill.: Charles C. Thomas, 1966.

Buck, Irving A., *Cleburne and His Command.* Ed. by Thomas Robson Hay. Dayton, Ohio: Morningside Bookshop, 1982.

Bull, Rice C., *Soldiering: The Civil War Diary of Rice C. Bull, 123rd New York Volunteer Infantry.* Ed. by K. Jack Bauer. San Rafael, Calif.: Presidio Press, 1977.

Carter, Samuel, III, *The Siege of Atlanta, 1864.* New York: Ballantine Books, 1973.

Cleaves, Freeman, *Rock of Chickamauga: The Life of General George H. Thomas.* Norman: University of Oklahoma Press, 1948.

Connolly, James A., *Three Years in the Army of the Cumberland: The Letters and Diary of Major James A. Connolly.* Ed. by Paul M. Angle. Bloomington: Indiana University Press, 1959.

Cox, Jacob D.:
The Battle of Franklin, Tennessee: November 30, 1864. New York: Charles Scribner's Sons, 1897.
The March to the Sea: Franklin and Nashville. New York: Charles Scribner's Sons, 1882.

Davis, Burke, *Sherman's March.* New York: Random House, 1980.

Develling, Charles Theodore, *History of the 17th Regiment, 1st Brigade, 3rd Division, XIV Corps.* Zanesville, Ohio: E. R. Sullivan, 1889.

Dickey, Thomas S., and Peter C. George, *Field Artillery Projectiles of the American Civil War.* Ed. by Floyd W. McRae Jr. Atlanta: Arsenal Press, 1980.

Edwards, William B., *Civil War Guns.* Secaucus, N.J.: Castle Books, 1962.

Evans, Clement A., ed., *Confederate Military History: A Library of Confederate States History, in Twelve Volumes.* Vol. 8. New York: Thomas Yoseloff, 1962.

Fleming, Walter L., comp. and ed., *General W. T. Sherman as College President.* Cleveland: Arthur H. Clark Co., 1912.

Foote, Shelby, *The Civil War, a Narrative: Red River to Appomattox.* New York: Random House, 1974.

Foster, Samuel T., *One of Cleburne's Command: The Civil War Reminiscences and Diary of Capt. Samuel T. Foster, Granbury's Texas Brigade, CSA.* Ed. by Norman D. Brown. Austin: University of Texas Press, 1980.

Franke, Norman H., *Pharmaceutical Conditions and Drug Supply in the Confederacy.* Madison, Wis.: American Institute of the History of Pharmacy, 1955.

Gibson, John M., *Those 163 Days: A Southern Account of Sherman's March from Atlanta to Raleigh.* New York: Coward-McCann, 1961.

Glatthaar, Joseph T., *The March to the Sea and Beyond.* New York: New York University Press, 1985.

Goldsborough, W. W., *The Maryland Line in the Confederate Army: 1861-1865.* Gaithersburg, Md.: Butternut Press, 1983 (reprint of 1900 edition).

Hartpence, Wm. R., *History of the Fifty-First Indiana Veteran Volunteer Infantry.* Harrison, Ohio: Privately published, 1894.

Hay, Thomas Robson, *Hood's Tennessee Campaign.* Dayton, Ohio: Morningside Bookshop, 1976.

Herr, George W., *Nine Campaigns in Nine States.* San Francisco: The Bancroft Co., 1890.

Hitchcock, Henry, *Marching with Sherman.* Ed. by M. A. DeWolfe Howe. New Haven: Yale University Press, 1927.

Hoehling, Adolf A., *Last Train from Atlanta.* New York: Thomas Yoseloff, 1958.

Hood, J. B., *Advance and Retreat: Personal Experiences in the United States & Confederate States Armies.* Ed. by Richard N. Current. Bloomington: Indiana University Press, 1959.

Horn, Stanley F.:
The Army of Tennessee. Norman: University of Oklahoma Press, 1941.
The Decisive Battle of Nashville. Knoxville: University of Tennessee Press, 1956.

Horn, Stanley F., comp. and ed., *Tennessee's War 1861-1865: Described by Participants.* Nashville: Tennessee Civil War Centennial Commission, 1965.

Johnson, Robert Underwood, and Clarence Clough Buel, eds., *Battles and Leaders of the Civil War.* Vol. 4. New York: Thomas Yoseloff, 1956 (reprint of 1887 edition).

Johnson, Rossiter, *Campfire and Battlefield: The Classic Illustrated History of the Civil War.* New York: The Fairfax Press, 1978 (reprint of 1894 edition).

Jones, Katharine M., *When Sherman Came: Southern Women and the "Great March."* New York: The Bobbs-Merrill Co., 1964.

Kerr, Laura E., *William Tecumseh Sherman: A Family Chronicle.* Lancaster, Ohio: Fairfield Heritage Association, 1984.

King, W. R., *Torpedoes: Their Invention and Use.* Washington, D.C.: U.S. Engineers Dept., 1866.

Kinnear, John R., *History of the 86th Illinois.* Chicago: Chicago Tribune Co., 1866.

Lawrence, Alexander A., *A Present for Mr. Lincoln: The Story of Savannah from Secession to Sherman.* Macon, Ga.: Ardivan Press, 1961.

Lewis, Lloyd, *Sherman: Fighting Prophet.* New York: Harcourt, Brace and Co., 1932.

Liddell Hart, B. H., *Sherman: Soldier, Realist, American.* Westport, Conn.: Greenwood Press, 1978.

McAllister, Anna, *Ellen Ewing: Wife of General Sherman.* New York: Benziger Brothers, 1936.

McDonough, James L., *Schofield: Union General in the Civil War and Reconstruction.* Tallahassee: Florida State University Press, 1972.

McDonough, James L., and Thomas L. Connelly, *Five Tragic Hours: The Battle of Franklin.* Knoxville: The University of Tennessee Press, 1983.

McMurry, Richard M., *John Bell Hood and the War for Southern Independence.* Lexington: The University Press of Kentucky, 1982.

Madaus, Howard Michael, *The Battle Flags of the Confederate Army of Tennessee.* Milwaukee: Milwaukee Public Museum, 1976.

Merrill, James M., *William Tecumseh Sherman.* Chicago: Rand McNally & Co., 1971.

Military Order of the Loyal Legion of the United States, Commandery of the District of Columbia. *War Papers.* Vol. 42. 1902.

Military Order of the Loyal Legion of the United States, Commandery of the State of Illinois, *Military Essays and Recollections:*
Vol. 2. Chicago: A. C. McClurg and Co., 1894.
Vol. 4. Chicago: Cozzens & Beaton, 1907.

Military Order of the Loyal Legion of the United States, Minnesota Commandery, *Glimpses of the Nation's Struggle:*
Fifth series. St. Paul: Review Publishing Co., 1903.
Sixth series. Minneapolis: Aug. Davis, 1909.

Neff, Cornelius, *Neal Neff's New National Poems, Composed by a Captain of the 54th O.V.V.I.* Cincinnati: Moore, Wilstach & Baldwin, 1866.

Pepper, George W., *Personal Recollections of Sherman's Campaigns in Georgia and the Carolinas.* Zanesville, Ohio: Hugh Dunne, 1866.

Perry, Milton F., *Infernal Machines: The Story of Confederate Submarine and Mine Warfare.* Baton Rouge: Louisiana State University Press, 1965.

Ridley, Bromfield L., *Battles and Sketches of the Army of Tennessee.* Dayton: Morningside Bookshop, 1978.

Sherman, William Tecumseh, *Memoirs of General William T. Sherman.* Bloomington: Indiana University Press, 1957.

Smith, George Winston, *Medicines for the Union Army.*

Madison, Wis.: American Institute of the History of Pharmacy, 1962.

Southern Historical Society Papers. Vols. 9 and 11. Millwood, N.Y.: Kraus Reprint Co., 1977.

Strong, Robert Hale, *A Yankee Private's Civil War.* Ed. by Ashley Halsey. Chicago: Henry Regnery Co., 1961.

United States War Department, *The Official Military Atlas of the Civil War.* Comp. by Calvin D. Cowles. New York: The Fairfax Press, 1983.

United States War Department, *The War of the Rebellion: A Compilation of the Official Records of the Union and Confederate Armies*, Series 1:

Vol. 45. Washington: GPO, 1894.

Additions and Corrections to Vol. 39. Washington: GPO, 1902.

Upson, Theodore F., *With Sherman to the Sea: The Civil War Letters, Diaries & Reminiscences of Theodore F. Upson.* Ed. by Oscar Osburn Winther. Baton Rouge: Louisiana State University Press, 1943.

Watkins, Sam R., *"Co. Aytch": A Side Show of the Big Show.* New York: Collier Books, 1962.

Williams, T. Harry:
Lincoln and His Generals. New York: Vintage Books, 1952.
P.G.T. Beauregard: Napoleon in Gray. Baton Rouge: Louisiana State University Press, 1955.

Wilson, James Harrison, *Under the Old Flag.* Vol. 2. Westport, Conn.: Greenwood Press, 1971.

Wood, George B., M.D., and Franklin Bache, M.D., *The Dispensatory of the United States of America.* Ed. by H. C. Wood, M.D. Philadelphia: J. B. Lippincott & Co., 1883.

Wyeth, John Allan, *Life of General Nathan Bedford Forrest.* Dayton, Ohio: Morningside Bookshop, 1975.

Other Sources

Castel, Albert, "The Life of a Rising Son." Parts 1-3. *Civil War Times Illustrated*, July, August, October 1979.

Civil War Times Illustrated. Special Nashville Campaign Edition, December 1964.

Coulter, S. L., "Battle of Franklin." *National Tribune*, December 28, 1882.

Horn, Stanley, "The Spring Hill Legend — A Reappraisal." *Civil War Times Illustrated*, April 1969.

Hoskinson, Stuart F., "Franklin." *National Tribune*, August 7, 1884.

McDonough, James Lee, "The General's Tour — The Battle at Franklin, Tennessee, November 30, 1864." *Blue & Gray Magazine*, August-September 1984.

Robison, Dan M., "The Carter House." *Tennessee Historical Quarterly*, March 1963.

PICTURE CREDITS

copied by Bill LaFevor — MASS-MOLLUS/USAMHI, copied by A. Pierce Bounds; South Caroliniana Library, University of South Carolina, copied by Charles E. Gay. 120: Courtesy Dr. Thomas P. Sweeney, photographed by Tom Davis — Tennessee State Museum, photographed by Bill LaFevor. 122: Kiefner-Kane Museum, Jefferson Barracks, Mo., photographed by Jack A. Savage; Alabama Department of Archives and History, photographed by John Scott. 124, 125: Courtesy Frank & Marie-T. Wood Print Collections, Alexandria, Va. 127: West Point Museum Collections, U.S. Military Academy, photographed by Henry Groskinsky; painting by Alexander Lawrie, West Point Museum Collections, U.S. Military Academy, photographed by Henry Groskinsky. 128, 129: Library of Congress. 131: Map by Walter W. Roberts. 132: Courtesy Frank & Marie-T. Wood Print Collections, Alexandria, Va. 133: MASS-MOLLUS/USAMHI, copied by A. Pierce Bounds. 135: Courtesy Frank & Marie-T. Wood Print Collections, Alexandria, Va. 136: Library of Congress — from *Nine Campaigns in Nine States*, by George W. Herr, published by The Bancroft Co., San Francisco, 1890, copied by A. Pierce Bounds. 138: Toledo-Lucas County Public Library, courtesy L. M. Strayer Collection. 140, 141: Library of Congress — Wide World; painting by Howard Pyle, courtesy Minnesota Historical Society, on loan to the Minnesota State Capitol, photographed by Gary Mortensen. 143, 145: Library of Congress. 146, 147: Courtesy Frank & Marie-T. Wood Print Collections, Alexandria, Va.; Library of Congress. 148, 149: L. M. Strayer Collection, copied by Brian Blauser — courtesy Frank & Marie-T. Wood Print Collections, Alexandria, Va. 151: Library of Congress. 152, 153: Courtesy Beverly M. DuBose Jr., photographed by Michael W. Thomas — Library of Congress; courtesy Frank & Marie-T. Wood Print Collections, Alexandria, Va. 154: Courtesy Frank & Marie-T. Wood Print Collections, Alexandria, Va. 155: New-York Historical Society. 157: Iowa State Historical Department. 158, 159: Courtesy Frank & Marie-T. Wood Print Collections, Alexandria, Va. 160, 161: Library of Congress — courtesy Frank & Marie-T. Wood Print Collections, Alexandria, Va. 162, 163: Courtesy Frank & Marie-T. Wood Print Collections, Alexandria, Va. — Special Collections Division, University of Georgia Libraries. 164-169: Courtesy Frank & Marie-T. Wood Print Collections, Alexandria, Va.

INDEX

Numerals in italics indicate an illustration of the subject mentioned.